What people are :

Elijah the Bodhisattva

In a beautiful meditation that exemplifies our interdependence, Malcolm Brown reflects on the life of Elijah, a forefather of monasticism in the West and one of the great Hebrew prophets, thru the striking lens of Buddhism and the Bodhisattva. Building a bridge that goes both ways, Brown's work enriches both Christianity and Buddhism, as well as the other traditions he engages. However, the greatest gifts herein lie for the spiritual practitioner. By placing an emphasis on the spiritual nature of a transformative path, Brown unearths tantalizing Biblical interpretations, with contemplations that roam across our religious traditions. In a world where traditional boundaries between religious traditions are being rapidly worn down in the existential lives of interspiritual practitioners, more books like this are needed — offering deep, respectful, and practice-oriented reflections between and among traditions. As an "unsystematic theology" that makes liberal use of "spiritual imagination," this book is a gem for anyone interested in interspirituality, new monasticism, spiritual practice, comparative theology, the essential interdependence of our contemplative traditions, or in being a better Christian or Buddhist — or simply a better human being.

Rory McEntee, co-author of *The New Monasticism: An Interspiritual Manifesto for Contemplative Living*

Malcolm Brown employs his wide knowledge of many faith traditions to create a kaleidoscopic interpretation of the Biblical story of Elijah. The prophet is seen in terms of Mahayana Buddhist concepts of nonduality and the Bodhisattva. This imaginative contribution to interfaith exegesis will enlighten some and exasperate others—or perhaps do both!

Ross Thompson, author of *Buddhist Christianity* and *The Interfaith Imperative*

Elijah the Bodhisattva

An Interspiritual Exploration

Elijah the Bodhisattva

An Interspiritual Exploration

Malcolm David Brown

BOOKS

Winchester, UK
Washington, USA

JOHN HUNT PUBLISHING

First published by O-Books, 2024
O-Books is an imprint of John Hunt Publishing Ltd., 3 East St., Alresford,
Hampshire SO24 9EE, UK
office@jhpbooks.com
www.johnhuntpublishing.com
www.o-books.com

For distributor details and how to order please visit the 'Ordering' section on our website.

Design: Lapiz Digital Services

UK: Printed and bound by CPI Group (UK) Ltd, Croydon, CR0 4YY
Printed in North America by CPI GPS partners

We operate a distinctive and ethical publishing philosophy in all areas of our business, from our global network of authors to production and worldwide distribution.

Contents

That of which we speak can never be found by seeking,
yet only seekers find it.
Bayazid Bistami

Introduction

Augustine allegedly said of Biblical interpretation that 'the more meanings the better'. This may be apocryphal, though I did find it in a nineteenth-century text,[1] so at least it predates the internet. In Jewish tradition, there are different 'levels' of interpretation—literal, 'hinted at', 'searched for', and esoteric[2]—but ultimately the Bible is about the inner life of God. Augustine really did argue that any understanding of the Bible must lead to a greater love of God and neighbor, or else it is a misunderstanding.[3] Inspired by Augustine, John Caputo defines religion as 'the love of God'. He doesn't say 'belief in God'; he says 'the love of God'. You might think it is impossible to love someone you don't believe in, but this paradox is really the whole point, for Caputo defines God as 'the becoming possible of the impossible'. A religious person is an 'unhinged lover' who loves the impossible made possible, and the opposite is a 'loveless lout' who is only concerned with the latest stock market figures. In this sense, an atheist or agnostic can be religious, and an adherent of Christianity, Judaism or Buddhism (for example) can be completely irreligious.[4]

In our globalized multicultural world, the love of neighbor means working to reconcile different spiritual traditions, not settling for a lowest common denominator but looking for ways in which they can enrich one another. This means investigating the foundations of the religions—Hans Küng said more than once there can be no peace among the nations without peace among the religions, no peace among the religions without dialogue between the religions, and no dialogue between the religions without investigation of the foundations of the religions.[5] It also means a negative dialectic of interpretation, in which 'the more interpretations the better' really does become a suitable ethos. In that spirit, I offer this 'interspiritual' commentary on the story of Elijah (1 Kings 17:1 to 2 Kings 2:13a in the Hebrew Bible, also known as the *Tanakh* and the Old Testament). By interspiritual, I mean I draw on the spiritual resources of different religions, treating them as resources to be nourished by, not as straitjackets in which to bind ourselves (*religare* in Latin). The commentary is inspired primarily by a Buddhist understanding, but also draws on Sufism and Quakerism,[6] as well as the Jewish and Christian traditions to which Elijah is more familiar. The key principle of my hermeneutic is to re-read (*relegere*) the externals of the story as internal to Elijah's mind, as he meanders toward enlightenment and ultimately realizes the non-duality of himself and God, YHWH, the ground of being-itself.

This may need some justification, but the story shows Elijah himself as compelled to reassess his boundaries, the boundaries of his religion. He thought YHWH was a henotheistic deity, a national God connected to the land of Israel, rather than the ground of being, being-itself, the God of those who struggle with God (the meaning of the name Israel). We see Elijah's ideas about God being gradually transformed and enlarged, though he goes backward as well as forward. Many key events in the story occur in liminal space, not quite part of the land of Israel, but not quite apart from it either.

The search for what religions have in common has recently become less popular. Perhaps the zeitgeist has gone back to a yearning for authenticity, in which each tradition must be understood in its own terms, anything else to be denounced as cultural appropriation. But the ground of being is beyond culture, and so is the love of God. It may be impossible to reconcile religious and spiritual traditions, but religion is a love of the impossible made real. Otherwise, the language of cultural authenticity can mask a crypto-fundamentalism, and remember that fundamentalism begins with an insistence that 'our' religion has certain fundamentals, certain non-negotiables. Blurring the boundaries is anti-essentialist, and this is essential! Nothing can have itself as a constituent part, which means (as Thich Nhat Hanh says) that Buddhism is made up *entirely* of non-Buddhist elements, Christianity of non-Christian elements, etc.[7] The Quaker *Advices and Queries* remind us that Christianity is not a notion but a way,[8] and the same is true of Buddhism, Judaism and other spiritual traditions. When the Abrahamic and dharmic religions appear to contradict each other, it may be we have missed something, however obvious or explicit the contradiction appears to us. More specifically, we need to be careful not to confuse the ontological with the experiential, or phenomenological. If Buddhist ontology says one thing and Jewish experience says another (or vice versa), that is not a contradiction. If there is a difference between Buddhist experience and Christian experience, again, that is fine. But sometimes there is a tendency to reify the experience, to 'ontologize' it, and this does lead into contradictions.

More practically, in our multicultural, multi-faith world, some of us will be brought up within one religious or spiritual tradition and then discover another, such as Buddhism. (People who are brought up Buddhist within a Western society might also develop a fascination with Christianity, and are probably uniquely placed to distinguish the *spiritual* path of Christianity from the broader Christian culture.) For such people, there seem to be three possibilities. The first is to convert. If you were a Christian, stop being Christian and start being Buddhist (or vice versa). The second is not to convert, but to practice Buddhism, or certain aspects of Buddhism, with a view to becoming a better Christian (again, or vice versa). The third is something more complex, a dual belonging, where you find it difficult to give a straight yes or no answer to questions like 'are you a Buddhist?' or 'are you a Christian?'

For the converts in particular, there is the danger of the comparative religion ego trap. For example, there can be a temptation to compare a Sunday school version of Christianity with a more sophisticated version of Buddhism, which of course makes Buddhism look more sophisticated. We can all fall into this trap from time to time—not just with religion—and there are a couple of indicators that might give us cause to stop and think. One is when we talk about spiritual paths in a dualistic way, using phrases such as 'Buddhist and non-Buddhist', 'Quaker and non-Quaker', 'Muslim and non-Muslim', etc. It *might* be that we're falling into the comparative religion ego trap if we're using such phrases. Not necessarily, but possibly. Another is when we start reifying the religions and spiritual paths: 'Buddhism teaches that...', 'Christianity believes that....' Actually, Buddhism doesn't have a mouth to teach with, so we're using this phrase to mean something else. Sometimes it might just be a convenient shorthand, but sometimes it's not.

For those who practice Buddhism to become better Christians, and others with some sort of dual belonging, there's a different hindrance. A common metaphor here is the well. If you want to dig a well, don't dig lots of shallow holes all over the place, but dig one hole, deeply. Now this metaphor might resonate with you. If it does, you should probably pay attention to it and ask yourself why. To practice one path might be good for you. It might be what you need, in which case you should probably stop reading this book now! But the metaphor of the well doesn't really do it for me, at least not in the way it's probably supposed to; I am more struck by the Hindu swami who said there's a difference between digging lots of wells and digging one well using lots of tools. We can also use tools from different tool sheds, and compare notes on tool maintenance with other tool owners, without abandoning the dream of digging a deeper well.

This same point is sometimes made with different metaphors. For example, different religions and spiritual practices are like pieces of a jigsaw—none of them contains the whole truth, so they really need to be combined, as in the Buddha's story of the blind men who were allowed to touch different parts of an elephant. One touched the ear, one the tusk, one the leg, one the tail, and so on, and then they argued with each other when asked to describe an elephant. Combining their insights would have been a better strategy.

The metaphors break down a bit in practice. Often what happens is that Christians think Buddhists have a piece of the puzzle they don't have, like meditation for example. But the encounter with Buddhism is precisely what enables them to discover teachings on meditation within their own tradition, practices such as *lectio divina*, the Ignatian spiritual exercises or the Jesus Prayer. Jesus was a Jewish Rabbi, and Jewish people also have discovered the richness of their own mystical traditions through an encounter with Buddhism,[9] and we encounter some of those traditions in this book. Such practices might be valuable for Buddhists as well. If you are a Buddhist and sometimes find yourself wondering whether to meditate or read, why not try *lectio divina*, which is a practice that combines the two?

When Buddhists are asked what pieces of the puzzle Christians have that they don't, they often say a social justice tradition. Of course, not all Christians are actively working for social justice, and some are frankly on the wrong side, but the tradition is there. Jesus doesn't say you can't follow God and Buddha, but he does say you can't serve God and mammon, which the New Testament identifies with the love of money and a cult of wealth, known today as capitalism. You can't realize *anatta*—the core Buddhist ontological principle of not-self—while putting yourself at the center. If Ayn Rand is right, and greed is good, then Christ and Buddha have both been defeated. So Jesus' teaching is diametrically opposed to prosperity theology, to the unholy alliance of Evangelicalism and Trumpism, to the new (and probably old) Constantinianism — be it concerned with money or with power. Like Elijah, it is sometimes necessary to spend time in the desert, traveling, being fed from a single cup of flour, being fed by ravens (which symbolize ritual uncleanness), rather than accommodating to the claimed lordship of Constantine. Whether this accommodation is for the purpose of defending conservative or progressive values is beside the point entirely — indeed, when it is for the purpose of defending progressive values an end-justifies-the-means mentality can become more tempting, more dangerous, and a greater betrayal of those same values.

Yet there is a real need for engaged Buddhism in today's world. It has been developed by thinkers and teachers as disparate as Ambedkar, Buddhadasa and Thich Nhat Hanh, and there are rich resources in the Abrahamic traditions that Buddhists can draw on, if they are willing to do so. Different pieces of the puzzle or not? I think Paul Knitter answers this question when he says that in order to know whether Christianity and Buddhism have more in common than we thought, 'we must not only pray and meditate together, but we must first act together with and for the oppressed.'[10] The phrase 'a preferential option for the poor' is sometimes used in liberation theology, and is even seen to be a characteristic of God, who 'has chosen the foolish things in the world to shame the wise, the weak to shame the strong, the things that are not to shame the things that are',[11] and this is seen in the story of Elijah, alongside and a part of his journey to enlightenment.

Rather than the jigsaw metaphor, it is possible to use a family tree metaphor. Religious and spiritual traditions are related to each other, they belong to the same family tree, which means they share a common ancestor, they have genetic material in common. Some argue the genetic material is something ethical, a variation on the Golden Rule for example. But the Golden Rule—to do unto others as you would have them do unto you—is more than an ethical slogan. Some people want to replace it with what they call the platinum rule—to treat others as they wish to be treated. But the Golden Rule has something the so-called platinum rule doesn't have, and that's what we have called *anatta*, not-self or no-self. The platinum rule is much more individualistic. The Golden Rule recognizes our interdependence much more. We might not be oppressed, but we're not different or separate from the oppressed either.

If I'm right about that, then the Buddhist concept of *anatta* is also taught in other religions, so it's possible to read Jewish or Christian texts through Buddhist eyes, and do so productively. Buddhism is the way of clarity—and this is essential if we are to demystify the concept of non-duality, for example, which is something that really needs to be done. Buddhism in turn can be enriched by the storytelling of the Abrahamic traditions. We can even say that some of the stories in the Hebrew Bible convey Buddhist insights in story form. The best example I can think of is in the story of Elijah, and it's what got me started on this book. In 1 Kings 19, Elijah is on the run from Ahab and Jezebel, he's hiding in a cave, and he's told to stand at the entrance of the cave, for YHWH is about to pass by. 'And YHWH passed by, and a great and strong wind tore the mountains apart and broke the rocks in pieces before YHWH, but YHWH was not in the wind; and after the wind an earthquake, but YHWH was not in the earthquake; and after the earthquake a fire, but YHWH was not in the fire; and after the fire a still silence-sound.' Isn't meditation often like that? The great dramatic epiphanies that come like a mighty wind, an earthquake, a fire; but the real insight is in the 'still silence-sound', the gentle whisper which is so quiet we don't know it's there, not until we've quietened ourselves.

Beyond the jigsaw and family tree metaphors, there are other ways of looking at these questions, and they have practical implications. Very briefly, Simone Weil said each religion *alone* is true, that is, it demands of us our complete and undivided attention,[12] by which she means the radical openness that Elijah needed to hear the gentle whisper. And there's also something more apophatic, to use a Greek Orthodox term. Some Christian thinkers have said that the more things we say God is not, the closer we get to what God is, because God is beyond human language—including the human language in the statement 'God exists'. This is also called the *via negativa*, and Buddhists often find it easier to grasp than Christians: to *believe* in nirvana, to *believe* in emptiness, is not to say they exist.[13] In one retreat I went on, the leader commented that every time we meditate we discover something new about what meditation is *not*. When we start out we think meditation is about emptying our minds, or becoming permanently blissful, and over the years we get a longer and longer list of things that meditation has turned out *not* to be. Maybe it was the same for Elijah, this process of elimination, this *via negativa*, leading him to enlightenment.

My interspiritual commentary may seem unsystematic, verging on a stream of consciousness with occasional contradictions—but *it is not a system*. In the story of Elijah, the system-builders are Ahab and Jezebel, the prophets of Baal and Asherah, and Ben-hadad, the Donald Trump of the Hebrew Bible. They're the bad guys in the story! When people impose a system on a revelation or a realization, it is not long before the system begins to take over. I don't think Christ and Buddha taught the same thing, but they have more in common with each other than either have with the religion that's named after them, and that's because they didn't teach a system, but a system is precisely what each religion has become. Maybe that's the difference between religion and spirituality. The commentary is a bit like the sort of spoken ministry you might expect to hear in a Quaker meeting, where people sit in silence and speak when they feel led to speak, 'out of the silence' which is 'where words come from'. Sentences and paragraphs sometimes follow each other in a manner analogous to Japanese *renga* poetry, in which the links 'depend mainly on the images of the stanzas, and on the psychic archetypes and actual situations from life which the images represent',[14] meaning that 'the greatest value or benefit from reading a *renga* comes from the reader's mind as he or she makes a completely personal journey from link to link.'[15] I can't avoid reading my own ideas, preoccupations, even prejudices into the text, but neither can anyone else. That's why Augustine was right when he said 'the more interpretations the better', and if he didn't really say it, then 'the more ways of loving God and neighbor the better' amounts to pretty much the same thing.

I hope there will be something, some insight, for the reader. It is an experiment in *un*systematic theology, more like a labyrinth than a straight line, so it is not an academic exegesis. I began by sitting quietly with the text, as though in a Quaker meeting, or doing a *lectio divina*. I aim for what Richard Rohr calls 'an alternative way of knowing that prayerfully *contemplates a text* instead of using it as dualistic ammunition',[16] and what Rodger Kamenetz calls 'a deeper way of reading: a way that performs a *tikkun* on the text, and finds the light hidden in the text'.[17] I don't treat academic insights as taboo, but I am more interested in engaging a 'spiritual imagination',[18] because the *via negativa* means that positive statements about God can only be made through analogy and metaphor. (And remember that metaphors and archetypes are *more* than literal, not less than literal.) In a finite world, the *via negativa* bridges an unbridgeable gap, which can only be bridged by personal experience.

So read this commentary slowly, and feel free to pause at any time. If it stimulates your own spiritual imagination, if it serves as a vehicle for your own thoughts and meditations, if it inspires your own interpretation of the metaphors and symbols, then it will have done its job, even if your insight is not what I had in mind when I wrote this, even if it leads us in opposite directions. We live on a globe, after all.

Unless otherwise stated, the text from the Hebrew Bible that is quoted in this commentary is my own reworking of the JPS[19] Tanakh (1917) translation, which is in the public domain.[20] Some of the reworking is merely an updating of language (e.g. changing 'thee' and 'thou' to 'you'), but sometimes I have gone further. I have not followed a consistent translation philosophy. Rather, I have rendered some phrases more literally, or stayed close to the JPS translation, especially when I want to make a point about the Biblical writer's choice of words. Where that is not the case, I have sometimes been more paraphrastic, and I have attempted to reflect some of the wordplay in the Hebrew. I have taken a similar approach to the few quotations from the New Testament, except these draw on various translations, including the Greek-English interlinear. If you want to consult a more expert translation, I recommend the New JPS Tanakh (1985) and/or the New Revised Standard Version (NRSV). Where I use technical terms from other languages (such as Pali, Sanskrit, Hebrew and Greek), I have usually avoided diacritical marks, but I have provided some references for anyone who wants to engage with the relevant scholarship, as well as primary sources and more 'popular' writing.

The Ground of Being (1 Kings 17)

If God is the becoming possible of the impossible, and the ground of being-itself, then it follows that the becoming possible of the impossible *is* the ground of being. Furthermore, if the Bible is ultimately about the inner life of God, then it follows that it is ultimately about the inner life of the becoming possible of the impossible, the inner life of the ground of being-itself. If that sounds confusing, then maybe it needs to be expressed in story form, such as the story we're about to encounter.

> **17** *Elijah the Tishbite, a sojourner in Gilead, said to Ahab: 'As YHWH the God of Israel lives, before whom I stand, there will be years without dew or rain, except according to my word.'* ² *The word of YHWH came to him and said:* ³ *'Leave here and go east, and hide yourself by the Cherith which flows into the Jordan.* ⁴ *You will drink from the stream, and I have commanded ravens to feed you there.'* ⁵ *So he went and did according to the word of YHWH, because he went and stayed by the Cherith which flows into the Jordan.* ⁶ *The ravens brought him bread and meat in the morning, and bread and meat in the evening, and he drank from the stream.*

The story begins with a drought, representing a dark night of the soul, when spiritual practice doesn't seem to bear any fruit at all. He is told to go to a valley leading to the Jordan, a place that is only ambiguously, if at all, part of the land of Israel. He is from Gilead, which is also a liminal place, on the margins, part but not part of the land of Israel. A lot of the Elijah story takes place on liminal ground. He is a sojourner, a resident alien in Gilead—not even a permanent inhabitant in that liminal space. He is a nomad, a spiritual seeker, someone journeying in the desert, who stops somewhere as at an oasis.

Elijah's name means 'my God is YHWH'. While his story is part of the Deuteronomic history, echoes of the earlier Yahwist author are frequent. YHWH, often translated into English as 'the LORD', is the ground of being,[1] existence itself, and is juxtaposed with El (translated 'God')—the first syllable of Elijah's name—throughout the Hebrew Bible. When the Cappadocian fathers said 'we believe in God, we do not say that God exists', and when Maimonides said 'there is no reality like his reality', there were pointing to YHWH as reality itself. It is not that God exists; God is existence itself. It is not that God is *a* being; God is being-itself. Reality as we perceive it is a shadow of YHWH, not the other way round. In the twentieth century, the view of God as the ground of being was associated with the theologian Paul Tillich, but being-itself is not an academic construct. It is the becoming possible of the impossible. It is love-itself, it is passionate, sometimes even messy. It has its roots in Moses' encounter with the burning bush, when he asked the deity he experienced 'what is your name?', and was told *'ehyeh asher ehyeh'*, I am what I am, I am who is, I am being-itself. The bush was burning, and yet it was not consumed. This is a perfect metaphor for the spiritual life—always burning but never consumed. Hence, Elijah is *you*, your spiritual journey as a seeker, a questioner. How could being-itself *not* be burning, and how could it ever be consumed?

Reality itself is personal and impersonal, and also interpersonal. The Three Jewels of Buddhism—the Buddha, the Dharma and the Sangha—represent this trinity. Although Dharma is impersonal, it is *experienced* as personal, as the ground of being, the burning bush, the empty tomb. Even the ground of being is a concept, a verbal reification, and there is no difference between squeezing God into a concept and squeezing God into an idol. They are necessary steps but they must be transcended, as the Torah reminds us again and again. We need to transcend the dualism of existence and non-existence. When

Anselm formulated his ontological argument for the existence of God, he reasoned that since God is, by definition, 'than which none greater can be conceived', and a God who existed in reality *and* in the imagination was greater than a God who existed in the imagination only, therefore a God who existed in reality was necessarily existent. But we can conceive of something greater than a God who exists in reality, and that is a God who transcends the dualism of existence and non-existence, who is the becoming possible of the impossible, being-itself, the ground of reality *and* of the imagination.

Thich Nhat Hanh says, 'God is the ground of being, but... not the being that is opposed to non-being. If it is the notion of being as opposed to non-being, then that is not God.'[2] In his translation of the Heart Sutra, he says the true nature of *all phenomena* is that of no being and no non-being. There is nothing mystical or mysterious about this. The ground of being is *necessarily, logically* beyond the dualism of existence and non-existence. So what is *not* God? How *can* we worship any God besides YHWH, the ground of being? What other objects of refuge are there besides the Three Jewels: the personal, the impersonal and the interpersonal? Yet as the story of Elijah shows, we sometimes forget this. Our journey, like his, is one of removing the obscurations and transforming them into factors of enlightenment.

Elijah speaks to Ahab, who at this stage represents the need to conform, to be all things to all people, not challenging himself or others. The expression 'as YWHW lives' is repeated as a refrain in the story of Elijah, and could be paraphrased 'as being-itself is', 'as existence exists'. However, there is also a repeated emphasis on YHWH being the God *of Israel*. This seems henotheistic, a form of cultural relativism, implying that what is good for other 'nations' (a word that is understood differently today) is not necessarily good for Israel, *and vice versa*. This henotheistic understanding is present in the text, but we also need to remember the meaning of the name Israel, as those who *struggle* with God (El). When Jacob wrestled with the angel after crossing the ford of the Jabbok,[3] which is near Elijah's nomadic encampment in Gilead, he was given this name. He was told he had struggled with Elohim, plural Gods rather than a singular God,[4] and the angel told Jacob (through a rhetorical question) that he must not ask his name, as God in the burning bush told Moses that he was being-itself, beyond naming conventions.

In the story of Elijah, there is a distinction between YHWH and 'the word of YHWH', which we see in this passage. It is a distinction, but not a duality. It hints at emanation, as in later Kabbalistic, Gnostic and Neoplatonist thought. The relationship between the word of YHWH and YHWH is also the relationship between the pointing finger and the moon. A Zen Buddhist teacher pointed at the moon and asked a pupil what it was, to which the pupil replied it was a finger. The point was that he missed the point. Sometimes God-talk takes us further from God, rather than closer. 'God hides pretty well in the word God,' says Rodger Kamenetz;[5] indeed, the one place in the universe where God is *most* hidden is the word God. This is why, as Jean-Christophe Rufin says in his book on the Camino de Santiago, Buddhism can bring us closer to God's essence. It is not *in spite* of not talking of God, but *because* of not talking of God.[6]

So we come closer to God in the unspoken, the unwritten, the *mindful* avoidance of the word 'God' and of the tetragrammaton, the replacement of YHWH with Adonai and Adonai with ha-Shem. The Jewish avoidance of pronouncing YHWH is an act of *mindfulness*, which I have tried to represent in this commentary. We can do this when we read the Elijah story out loud. If we forget to replace YHWH with Adonai, we return to the beginning of the chapter or section we were reading. This is like the practice of counting the breath in meditation—when we lose count, we simply return to the number one, without judging ourselves. When we watch the breath and then lose concentration, we simply bring our attention back, gently. It is not a forfeit, a self-imposed punishment. It is the practice itself, and new layers of meaning get revealed as we start from the beginning again and again.

Most translations say Elijah is fed by ravens, though it has been speculated that the word might mean Arabians. There is deliberate ambiguity, wordplay and punning throughout the Elijah story. Either way, spiritual friendship is more significant than kinship, nationality or even species membership. The Buddha's disciple Ananda famously remarked that spiritual friendship seemed to be half of the spiritual path, to which the Buddha replied it was the *whole* of the spiritual path.

The raven is an unclean animal, which does not provide for its young, causing them to 'cry unto God, they wander for lack of meat', according to the book of Job.[7] Although the ravens provide meat for Elijah, it is a different word in Hebrew. In Job it is *okel* (meat, food, prey), while here it is *basar* (flesh, even flesh that is torn from carrion). This draws attention to the unclean nature of the food, emphasizing that ritual purity is less important than meditative absorption, a oneness with God and with all that is (YHWH). In the New Testament, John the Baptist told people with food to share with people who had none,[8] but he also used a word for food that was not ritually clean. Elijah's meditative absorption is highlighted by his drinking from the oasis-like stream, reminiscent of Gideon who accepted as his soldiers only those who drank in mindfulness.[9]

[7] *A while later the stream dried up, because there was no rain in the land.* [8] *The word of YHWH came to him and said:* [9] *'Get up and go to Zarephath, which belongs to Sidon, and stay there. I have commanded a widow there to provide for you.'*

The text says Zarephath 'belongs to Sidon', not that it is 'part of Sidon'. It too is a liminal place, a border town at the frontier of Canaan and Phoenicia, which was the home of Baal. This is a challenge to Elijah's henotheism, the beginning of his movement to monotheism and ultimately to a non-dual realization that there is nothing but God. A *widow*, a poor person, has been commanded to provide for Elijah; a spiritually poor person has been commanded to feed him spiritually.

What does it mean for a spiritual friend or teacher to be *spiritually* poor? It means what Origen called *apocatastasis* — ongoing, eternal progress, the recognition of a never-ending need to learn. It means humility, a willingness to receive as well as give. The widow of Zarephath is willing to share what little she has with Elijah, and by the end of the chapter she is also willing to receive. The spiritually poor means those whose spirits are crushed, either because of material poverty and a desperate yearning for social justice (as we see later), or because they have become conscious of the suffering, the *dukkha*, that the Buddha tells us is an ontological mark of existence, inseparable from life. In the Psalms we read the experiential statement that YHWH is near to those who have a broken heart and saves those who have a crushed spirit.[10] In becoming an interspiritual teacher, Mirabai Starr drew on her own grief, and she cites a grief counselor who also went through great losses.[11] It is emphatically not that such suffering is to be desired as a way to become a teacher, but what suffering we *do* experience has the potential to lead us to *empathy*, as well as the opposite potential of us sinking into hard-heartedness. On the subject of *tonglen* — the Tibetan practice of exchanging self with other — Pema Chödron writes:

When you feel the discomfort, have the thought: 'Other people feel this.' And then if you want to take it a rather dramatic step further, you can say, 'May we all be free of this.' But it's enough just to acknowledge that other people feel this pain. And the most dramatic and probably most difficult step is to say: 'Since I'm feeling this anyway, may I be feeling it so all others could be free of it.' So tonglen meditation has three levels of courage. The first is to say, 'Other people feel this.' And that is enough. But if, in that particular moment of time, it feels genuine to say, 'May this become a path for awakening the hearts of all of us,' do so. And the one that takes you to the deepest level of courage is: 'Since I'm feeling this anyway, may I feel it so that others could be free of it'.[12]

This applies to more than formal meditation practice. In finding our vocation, our path in life, Andrew Harvey advises us to follow our heartbreak,[13] to ask which of the world's wrongs affect us most deeply and resolve to do something about them. This is not opposed to following our bliss (Joseph Campbell), or to asking what makes us come alive and doing that, since what the world needs is people who have come alive (Howard Thurman). It is complementary and overlapping. Your vocation will be found at the point where the answers to these three questions intersect: what is your heartbreak; what is your bliss; what makes you come alive?

[10] *So Elijah got up and went to Zarephath, and when he arrived at the gate of the city a widow was gathering sticks there. He called her and said: 'Please get me a small cup of water, so I can drink.'*

The widow is at the *gate* of the town, yet again a liminal place. It is like a tip-of-the-tongue moment—the realization is there but she hasn't quite realized it's there! And neither has Elijah, who is also at this threshold. The widow is 'gathering sticks', symbolizing a 'foraging' approach to meditation or spiritual realization. Not knowing we're in a forest, we search around for sticks. The Buddhist book *Zen Flesh, Zen Bones* quotes Sufi master Inayat Khan recounting a Hindu story of a fish who goes to a queen fish to ask about this thing called the sea. No doubt the fish had already asked other fish, including older, wiser ones, and been told the sea was far, far away, or that only credulous and senile old fish believed it even existed. But the queen fish explained: 'You live, move, and have your being in the sea. The sea is within you and without you, and you are made of sea, and you will end in sea. The sea surrounds you as your own being.'[14] As Epimenides said of Zeus, and the apostle Paul later said of God, 'In him we live and move and have our being.'[15] The Sufi sheikh Bayazid Bistami also said the thing of which we speak can never be found by seeking, yet only seekers find it, and there's another Zen story of a master who polished a stone, claiming he was trying to make it into a mirror, to highlight that you couldn't become a Buddha through meditation. There are many ways of saying this.

[11] *As she was going to fetch the cup of water, he called to her and said: 'Please also bring me a piece of bread.'* [12] *She said: 'As YHWH your God lives, I do not have any cake, only a handful of flour in the jar and a little oil in the jug. I am gathering two sticks, so I can go inside and cook something for me and my son, so we can eat it and die.'* [13] *Elijah said to her: 'Do not be afraid. Go and do what you said, but first make me a small loaf and bring it to me, and then cook for you and your son,* [14] *because YHWH the God of Israel says this: "The jar of flour will not be used up and the jug of oil will not run dry until the day that YHWH sends rain on the land."'* [15] *She went and did what Elijah had said, and she and he and her household ate for many days.* [16] *The jar of flour was not used up and the jug of oil did not run dry, according to the word of YHWH which was spoken by Elijah.*

Elijah's henotheism is tentative but still present—YHWH alone is to be worshipped *in the land of Israel*. The widow respects that Elijah's God is YHWH (as his name indicates) with the words 'as YHWH *your* God lives'. Elijah asks her to bring him a piece of bread, not a cake, but she doesn't think she has anything worth giving. By asking for her teachings, and accepting them, Elijah helps her to realize she is a teacher. She has already brought water to Elijah, and done so happily, but when he asks for food she is more reluctant. She has second-hand knowledge she is happy to share, but she believes she has nearly exhausted her own inner wisdom, the knowledge given to her by her *inner* teacher, and is on the verge of giving up.

She intends to prepare food 'so we can eat it and die'. Later in the story, Elijah also wants to die. This symbolizes giving up on the spiritual quest, but it is when the dark night of the soul reaches its darkest that the dawn is about to break. The Ramadan fast begins when the white thread of dawn is distinguishable from the black thread.[16] The dark night of the soul is a struggle, and the struggle does not bring realization. It is the letting go that allows grace to come through. This often happens in meditation practice; the meditation itself seems to lead nowhere, but when we stop and relax, when we take our bags back to the car after a discouraging retreat, that is when the realization comes. We cannot make a mirror by polishing a tile, and we can never reach enlightenment by meditating. That of which we speak can never be found by seeking, yet only seekers find it.

Elijah tells the widow that the flour and oil will not run out. A simple practice, like reciting a mantra, can yield results and continue to yield results. In J. D. Salinger's novel *Franny and Zooey*, Franny says that frequent repetition of the Jesus prayer — 'Lord Jesus Christ, son of God, have mercy on me' — causes it to become 'self-active', and that the same is true of Buddhist mantras such as the *nianfo* or *nembutsu* (homage to the Buddha Amida), and the even simpler practice of simply repeating the name (or names) of God. This, she observes, is a teaching found in many spiritual traditions. In the same way, the widow is willing to share what little she has and *as a result, because of that,* it never runs out. She isn't promised or given more resources, but what she has lasts. The spiritual path seems to have a habit of making us materially poor but somehow never running out. The burning bush never stopped burning, and yet it was never consumed. The willingness of a boy to share his five loaves and two fishes allowed Jesus to feed five thousand men, plus women and children. Those who have walked the Camino de Santiago will know the phrase 'the Camino provides'. In the widow's case, as in every case, it is really a result of grace, but her generosity and lack of self-preservation lower the barriers to grace she put up earlier, and that come across in her initial reply to Elijah—though even this reply shows that her clinging to self-preservation has already been lessened, albeit in the form of giving up. Our obscurations and imperfections are like clouds, barriers to grace, and our true Buddha-nature is like the sky, grace.

In Buddhist circles, there can be an aversion to the word 'grace', sometimes because it is seen as too Christian, reflecting a dualism of Abrahamic and dharmic paths. But Marco Pallis argues that 'the idea of "grace"…is by no means unintelligible in the light of Buddhist teachings.' It is explicit in Pure Land Buddhism, but also implicit in early Buddhism, Mahayana and Vajrayana. When the Buddha says, 'There is, O monks, an unborn', his words are 'plainly couched in the language of transcendence; any Christian or Muslim could have used these same words when referring to God and the world. This transcendence is propounded by the sutra as providing real grounds for human hope.' Furthermore, the *'attractive* influence of enlightenment' is 'experienced as providential and merciful *emanation* from the luminous center' and *'strikes* on human consciousness'.[17]

Of the names of God in Islam, Pallis observes a similarity with two *yidams* of Tibetan Vajrayana Buddhism:

Ar-Rahman refers to God's clemency as an intrinsic quality of the Divine Being, whereas *Ar-Rahim* refers to that quality as projected into the creation. It expresses the dynamic aspect of clemency, mercy poured forth and reaching creatures in the form of grace as well as in other ways. Like the Buddhist compassion, it has a dynamic quality, it must find an object for its exercise. It is easy to see that these two names respectively correspond, in all essentials, to Amitabha and Chenrezig.[18]

The words 'until the day that YHWH sends rain on the land' could almost make it seem as if the rain is something to be afraid of. The food would need to start growing again and it wouldn't be instantly available, though of course there would be water to drink. But if we look at it in terms of spiritual practice then this *one* practice, such as reciting a mantra, which lasts 'for many days', gives way to something more pluralistic, a discovery that the one-pointed practice has served its purpose and is no longer needed. When Franny said the Jesus prayer became self-active, she was referring to the anonymous nineteenth-century Russian book *The Way of a Pilgrim*: 'Early one morning somehow the prayer awakened me'.[19] We reach the point of being stream-enterers, where our progress toward the sea is irreversible, where we have enough in the tank to keep ourselves going until we reach enlightenment, a complete realization of emptiness, the state of an *arahant* or a Buddha.

What is the 'something more pluralistic' to which the one-pointed practice gives way? It is interspiritual practice, a realization of the non-duality of spiritual practice and the reality to which spiritual practice refers. There are not many paths to God, but there is no path that is not a path to God. In response to the accusation that interspiritual practice is like digging lots of shallow wells rather than one deep one, Episcopal priest Matthew Wright quotes a Hindu swami, who said to him,

'Matthew, there's a difference between digging fifteen shallow wells and using fifteen tools to dig one.'[20]

[17] *After these things, the son of the woman who was the mistress of the house became sick, so sick that there was no breath left in him.* [18] *She said to Elijah: 'What have I to do with you, man of God? Have you come to remind me of my sin, and cause my son to die?'* [19] *He said to her: 'Give me your son.' He took him out of her arms and carried him into the upper chamber where he was staying, and laid him on his own bed.* [20] *He cried out to YHWH: 'YHWH my God, have you brought evil on the widow I am staying with, causing her son to die?'* [21] *He stretched himself out on the child three times, and cried out to YHWH: 'YHWH my God, please let this child's soul come back into him.'* [22] *YHWH heard the voice of Elijah, and the soul of the child came back into him, and he lived.* [23] *Elijah brought the child down from the upper chamber into the house, handed him to his mother and said: 'See, your son is alive.'* [24] *And the woman said to Elijah: 'Now I know you are a man of God, and the word of YHWH in your mouth is truth.'*

When the text says there is no *breath* left in him, this does not simply mean his lungs have stopped functioning and he is therefore physically dead. The Hebrew word *neshama*, like the Sanskrit *prana*, the Tibetan *lung*, the Greek *pneuma*, the Chinese *qi* or *ch'i* and no doubt equivalent words in other languages, refers to the spirit *and* the breath. It does not distinguish between them. It is the spirit *riding* on the breath. That the same concept exists in so many languages suggests it refers to something deep in the human experience.

Thich Nhat Hanh has written deeply and extensively on mindfulness of breathing, and it is one of the most established and widespread meditation practices. The Buddha taught it in some detail in both the Satipatthana Sutta and the Anapanasati Sutta, suggesting it could lead to clear vision in this lifetime, and liberation from *samsara*, the suffering of cyclic existence. Sometimes I get frustrated with meditating on the breath, because it feels narcissistic, but the breath is miraculous, something to be profoundly grateful for, and when I realize this, it is not difficult to be mindful of it.

The widow has accepted her responsibility as Elijah's teacher, so she is now called 'the mistress of the house', but she thinks her misfortune is a punishment, a consequence of the bad karmic seeds she has sown. Perhaps this is a natural misunderstanding, but when we realize the laws of karma mark our *experience*, in contrast to the three marks of *existence*, or ontology, that include *anatta*, not-self, then this misunderstanding starts to be cleared away. Her anguished cry to Elijah can be compared to someone asking the Buddha why he talked about suffering so much, as though he had brought suffering on people. The Buddha's purpose was to help people *recognize* their suffering, because it is only *after* we recognize our suffering that it can come to an end. We experience this on a smaller scale in meditation. People often say they begin meditating and feel more distracted and angrier than before. But that is a sign of progress. They are not really more distracted and angrier; they are more *aware* of their distractions and anger.

Elijah takes the child to the 'upper chamber', a significant phrase that is repeated toward the end of his story. It seems unlikely that a poor person's house in that time and place would have two stories with an inside set of stairs, like many middle-class houses in Western countries today. Maybe there would be an outside stairway to a flat roof. The upper chamber could have been a hut, something a shepherd would have slept in. It is also symbolic of our higher nature, our higher calling, a simplicity the other side of complexity. It is outside the main dwelling, even of a person who is materially and spiritually poor, so it symbolizes a removal of oneself for the purpose of quiet, stillness, meditation. But this is temporary. As the Sufi

Sheikh Abu Sa'id said, the 'true saint goes in and out among the people and eats and sleeps with them and buys and sells in the market and marries and takes part in social intercourse, and never forgets God for a single moment.'[21]

He stretches over the child three times. On one level, this is an indication of Elijah's great emotion, as though he hugged the child's corpse three times. However, a lot of things in the story of Elijah, and in other spiritual texts, are done in threes. As with the Trinity in Christianity, and the Triple Gem or Three Jewels in Buddhism, it is a representation of the personal, the impersonal and the interpersonal. He stretches out three times. The first is personal, for himself, because he is afraid he has been made to look foolish or a fraud. The second is for the child, as Elijah recognizes the interpersonal relationship between them. This is a moment of true altruism. Elijah is offering to exchange his own life for the child's. This is relative *bodhicitta*—Elijah is only part-way there. Many of us have experienced this, attempting to 'bargain' for the life of a dog, for example. It is *bodhicitta*, but it is relative *bodhicitta*. The realization of *anatta* is a different thing, where Elijah and the child become inseparable. So the third stretching out is for a non-dual transcendence, where there is no room for anything but God. This is an intimation of absolute *bodhicitta*, beyond the relative (but still significant) *bodhicitta* of the second stretch, the second stage. It is then that the boy is healed.

Similarly, with the Jesus prayer, the Camino and the fast of Ramadan, there is an initial stage that is predominantly physical. We say the prayer with the lips, we experience physical discomfort in the legs and feet, we feel hungry and experience disruption to sleep. This is followed by a mental or emotional stage—often characterized by boredom or increased mental chatter. Doing the Camino, I started wishing for the earlier physical discomfort as a way of driving out the mental chatter. We should be careful what we wish for. But eventually there is a third stage, a spiritual or meditative one. The prayer prays itself inside the practitioner. The Camino and the pilgrim become one, seen, as it were, from a God's-eye perspective. The fast really does produce the fruit of *taqwa*—God-consciousness or mindfulness—experienced as remembrance of God and other people who are fasting voluntarily or involuntarily, as gratitude, as connection with nature, as an increasing freedom from habitual patterns of behavior.

Elijah and the child become inseparable because non-self and non-duality are closely related. If there is not a duality of self and other, of *brahman* and *atman*, then there is no self, no *atman*. The child's *soul* is returned because the child is no longer separate. The Buddha's teaching on *anatta* is not a refutation of Hindu doctrine, but a clarification and application. It is essentially *advaita*, though even *dvaita*, as practiced in *bhakti* devotion, can be a path to *advaita*. There is also an apophatic element here. Marco Pallis writes that *anatta* is to be seen in the context of non-duality and through an apophatic method, which is why he is critical of the notion that Buddhism is 'atheistical'.[22] Rather, *anatta* is a middle way between theism and non-theism, or, better, a non-dual transcendence of theism and non-theism. It is the same non-dual transcendence we saw Anselm unwittingly point us toward with his ontological argument, toward a God who is being-itself, who transcends the duality of existence and non-existence.

The text also emphasizes that Elijah lays the child *on his own bed*. By doing this, and stretching his body over the child, Elijah symbolically shares his merit with the child. In Buddhist teaching, the sharing of merit creates merit, because it is a recognition of non-self. Elijah's stretching was also a form of prostration. There is a link here between body and mind— meditation practice and even enlightenment itself are *embodied*. In Christian language, this is called incarnation.

Paolo Coelho, in his novel *The Fifth Mountain*, suggests Elijah may have been in love with the widow. The point is not whether Coelho is right or wrong here—it is a novel after all—but that Elijah's partial love is transformed into something transcendent. Emotion is not separate from embodiment or from meditation or prayer. There is a wholeness here. And yet, the widow says: 'Now I know...the word of YHWH *in your mouth* is truth.' She has made progress toward a direct perceptual realization of ultimate reality, of emptiness, but she is still experiencing at second hand. A glimpse of enlightenment, from however far away, is a thrilling moment, but it is not the center of the labyrinth. Indeed, the biggest obstacle can be the temptation to think we have reached the end of the journey. When Shams met Rumi and asked who was greater, Bayazid who said 'Glory to me, how great is my majesty', or Muhammad who said 'We do not know you as we should', Rumi replied that Bayazid was content with a glimpse of divine glory, but Muhammad's thirst for God was without limit. This was his spiritual poverty, his *apocatastasis*. According to Sogyal Rinpoche:

> The spiritual journey is one of continuous learning and purification. When you know this, you become humble. There is a famous Tibetan saying: 'Do not mistake understanding for realization, and do not mistake realization for liberation.' And Milarepa said: 'Do not entertain hopes for realization, but practice all your life.'[23]

The child comes *down* from the upper chamber, from the mountaintop to the valley, from meditative absorption to the marketplace. It is significant that this is a child. In Jungian analysis, the archetype of the child represents 'who we really are and how we would most authentically express ourselves if there were no inhibiting factors',[24] such as social norms and expectations (the *animus*), or calculations of what is good for us (the *anima*). The New Testament urges its readers to 'become like children', 'long for pure, spiritual milk', and even 'be born again',[25] a phrase that has been much misunderstood and misrepresented. Like the *myokonin* of Pure Land Buddhism,[26] the beginner's mind (*shoshin* in Japanese) is praised in Zen Buddhism, because: 'In the beginner's mind there are many possibilities, but in the expert's mind there are few.'[27]

Samsara (1 Kings 18:1–19)

18 After many days, in the third year, the word of YHWH came to Elijah: 'Go and show yourself to Ahab, because I will send rain on the land.' ² Elijah went and showed himself to Ahab. The famine was especially bad in Samaria.

The phrase 'in the third year' is repeated later, and highlights the way things are done in threes. It is really a basic structure of human experience, formalized in philosophy as thesis–antithesis–synthesis. We have already seen this structure in the form of personal–impersonal–interpersonal. The three years of Jesus' ministry are sometimes identified as the year of obscurity, the year of popularity, and the year of opposition,[1] and as Jung says: 'What happens in the life of Christ happens always and everywhere.'[2]

'After many days...the word of YHWH came to Elijah.' The tone suggests Elijah is tired of waiting, beginning to wonder if mindfulness was a waste of time and enlightenment was a myth. Perhaps he isn't a prophet after all. In Mahayana Buddhism, there is a story of the bodhisattva Avalokiteshvara, also known as Chenrezig and as Guan Yin, momentarily losing hope when faced with all the suffering in the world, and shattering into many pieces. But the Buddha Amitabha enabled Avalokiteshvara to have eleven heads to hear the cries of sentient beings, and a thousand arms with which to help them. Elijah has waited and waited, and the next step might seem difficult, but he faces up to his responsibilities and his vocation by showing himself to Ahab.

YHWH promises to 'send rain on the land'. If the Hebrew word here was *eretz*, it would mean specifically the land that is identified with the presence of God. God would be about to nourish the place that is identified with the divine presence,

God encountering God, as the Jesus prayer begins to pray itself, as the stream-enterer of Theravada Buddhism is on a one-way journey toward enlightenment and liberation. However, in this case the Hebrew word is not *eretz* but *adamah*. These are often used as near-synonyms, but *adamah* is related to Adam, and means the dust from which he was formed. It could almost be translated as sending rain upon the dust, or the dusty earth, a real indication of quenching. *Eretz* is like *Gaia*, while *adamah* is like soil. A minister friend of mine said of the publican's prayer—God be merciful to me a sinner[3]—that he didn't have a sense of God's passionate womb-like (*rahem* in Hebrew) healing mercy (*eleos* in Greek, alluding to medicinal olive oil), but a more judicial sense of forgiveness, yet even that was enough for him to be forgiven and justified. Here, the rain is not sent on the *eretz* but on the *adamah*, yet this is enough. The term *tathagatagarbha* (Buddha-nature) also includes the word for 'womb': to 'have' the Buddha-nature is to be the womb of a Buddha, yet becoming a stream-enterer is enough and will eventually lead to the *eretz* of nirvana (*rahem*).

'The famine was especially bad in Samaria', the capital of the northern kingdom of Israel, the center of political power and clinging to the delusions of selfhood, so of course the spiritual famine is severe there. ('Samaria' and 'samsara' are fortuitously similar words.) It is easier for a camel to pass through the eye of a needle than for the rich and powerful to enter the kingdom of heaven, says Jesus. In contrast to Ahab, Elijah's politics are the politics of *anatta*, not-self. Immediately after the story of Elijah ends, we read that Samaria is where his successor Elisha's ministry begins. This symbolizes going back to where others have been, then moving on to seek enlightenment at first hand. When the Zen Master Joshu was asked for the secret of enlightenment, he replied: 'I have to go take a pee now. It's silly, isn't it? Such a little thing. And yet one must do it in person.'[4]

³ Ahab called Obadiah, who was in charge of the household. Obadiah feared YHWH greatly, ⁴ for when Jezebel persecuted the prophets of YHWH, Obadiah took a hundred of them, hid fifty in one cave and fifty in another, and he fed them with bread and water. ⁵ Ahab said to Obadiah: 'Go through the land, to all the springs and all the valleys. Perhaps we will find grass to keep the horses and mules alive, so we will not have to kill all the animals.' ⁶ So they divided the land between them and went in opposite directions. Ahab went one way by himself, and Obadiah went another way by himself. ⁷ While Obadiah was on the way, Elijah met him, and he recognized him and fell on his face and said: 'Is it you, my lord Elijah?' ⁸ He answered him: 'It is I. Go tell your lord that Elijah is here.'

It is interesting that Obadiah holds such a position of trust. There is something of a *yin-yang* here, a 'spot' of nirvana in the 'center' of samsara. In Jewish tradition, he is identified with the writer of the Biblical book of Obadiah. There is probably some symbolism here, especially if the book of Kings was written after the book of Obadiah. So why is the prophet Obadiah written into the text here, especially as a not-yet-fully-formed prophet? Clearly, Obadiah is not an Elijah. His fear of YHWH is greater than his love for YHWH. Yet his fear of YHWH is also greater than his fear of Jezebel. He is focused on something more spiritual than Ahab, who is fixated on material security, keeping his horses and mules alive while people around him are dying from the drought. It is not that animals are unworthy of concern, but they symbolize what Sufis call the *nafs*, a clinging to the lower self. Ahab wants and expects Obadiah to participate in this clinging. So Obadiah is not a bodhisattva, but more of an Ananda. This goes well with his name, which means 'servant of God', like the Arabic Abdullah. As Ananda is the servant of the Buddha, so Obadiah is the servant of God, and he addresses Elijah with humility. In the interaction between Ahab and Obadiah it is only Ahab who is quoted, whereas Obadiah and Elijah are immediately in dialogue with one another. If Obadiah is like Ananda, then Elijah is like the Buddha (or rather Siddhartha Gautama before he became the Buddha), and Ahab is like the Buddha's father or even Mara, symbolizing the temptation to chase after power, or wealth, or beauty, even if it can be used for good—*especially* if it can be used for good. Ahab doesn't imagine he needs to listen to Obadiah, but later he will listen to Elijah.

But Obadiah plays another role. As we soon learn, Elijah believes he is the only prophet of YHWH left, but Obadiah has saved a hundred prophets of YHWH. Jezebel's persecution symbolizes dualism and self-grasping gaining the upper hand, seemingly destroying the goodness, the Buddha-nature. But it is still there, hiding in a cave—indeed two caves—being kept alive with bread and water. Bread and water may not sound like much, but when Siddhartha Gautama ate a small bowl of rice and milk, it was enough to keep him going to the end. This theme re-emerges later.

Like Abraham and Lot,[5] Obadiah and Ahab go in opposite directions. Obadiah goes in the direction of Elijah, because his spiritual path leads him in that direction, to be more like Elijah, to be a prophet in his own right. Ahab can't find Elijah without Elijah's grace—which he receives from YHWH—and Obadiah's help. To find enlightenment we need both grace and assistance. So Ahab and Obadiah take different paths, but in many ways this is a wise thing to do. Excessive individualism can be a hindrance, but conforming to the norms of a community can be a greater one. There is a spiritual as well as political significance in the Quaker advice to 'Respect the laws of the State but let your first loyalty be to God's purposes.'[6]

Elijah meets him, which is an instance of grace, and Obadiah recognizes him, that is, he sees a glimpse of enlightenment. It is a second-hand glimpse of enlightenment because it wasn't a direct encounter with YHWH. Even so, Obadiah falls on his

31

face as Abraham fell before YHWH and Lot fell before the angels in Sodom,[7] shielding his face because even this second-hand glimpse seems momentarily overwhelming. At this point, Obadiah relates to Elijah as Elijah relates to YHWH. Obadiah refers to Elijah as his 'lord', then Elijah tells him to tell his 'lord' that Elijah is here. It seems Elijah is being a bit unfriendly, not really believing Obadiah is on the side of the prophets of YHWH. Sometimes spiritual practice seems to make us worse before it makes us better. But has Obadiah really chosen his path yet? Maybe Elijah needs to learn some compassion toward Obadiah's hesitation, his lack of commitment. Indeed, the dialogue teaches them both: Elijah becomes more patient and compassionate, while Obadiah becomes more courageous and committed, like Gautama when he vows to stay under the tree for as long as it takes.

[9] *He said: 'How have I sinned? Why would you send your servant back to Ahab? He will kill me.* [10] *As YHWH your God lives, there is no nation or kingdom to which my lord has not sent someone to look for you, and when they said you were not there, he made them swear an oath that they were unable to find you...'*

Obadiah's understanding of karma is like the widow's was earlier, not understanding that karma is a mark of experience while *anatta* is a mark of existence. Both of them use the word 'sin', which has an exclusively religious meaning in modern English, but a much more everyday meaning in the ancient world. Sometimes it is said that Buddhism does not have a concept of sin, rather one of ignorance, but this juxtaposition shows a misunderstanding of sin before it was turned into a religious word. It is not the same as evil, or rule-breaking, still less an original defilement transmitted from generation to generation. It refers to an archer missing the bullseye but hitting the target, or a hunter wounding an animal but failing to kill it cleanly. This would result in a painful, drawn-out death, and the tribe still wouldn't be fed. When the Psalmist says 'Against you, you only, have I sinned',[8] he acknowledges he has wounded God and only God, in that he has divided the unity of being-itself into a duality of self and other. He has been ignorant of his true nature, and this has caused suffering. His cry is a very Buddhist one. The New Testament makes the same point when it defines sin as whatever does not come from faith.[9] It is what the Quaker writer Parker Palmer calls a 'functional atheism',[10] a belief or attitude that it all depends on *me*.

Obadiah uses the expression 'YHWH *your* God'. He may have been discouraged by Elijah's unfriendliness, but Elijah is not completely wrong, because Obadiah is still serving two masters. Having referred to Elijah as 'my lord', he now refers to Ahab as 'my lord'. Ahab has searched everywhere, but he is a superficial seeker, not willing to pay attention to the signs on the path, not having the patience to follow the *via negativa*, the path of saying 'God is not this', 'God is not this', gradually coming to a greater realization of what God is. Ahab could never find his heart's true desire by seeking, yet neither would he find it without *truly* being a seeker. He is like the hungry ghost in the Tibetan mandala who sits on top of a storeroom full of food, peering into the distance in search of something to eat. Obadiah, on the other hand, has had a glimpse of enlightenment, nirvana, salvation, eternal bliss, and is immediately told to go back to Samaria as a messenger, like the arhat in Mahayana Buddhism who is awakened from *samadhi* and sent back to samsara as a bodhisattva. Understandably he puts up some resistance. Until recently he has been a trusted servant of Ahab, and now he expects to be killed at any time.

Ahab's demand for an oath implies arrogance, as though he is in a position to make demands of other kings, who are his equals. It also implies a double standard of truth, which is why Quakers and some others have historically refused to swear oaths. What Ahab represents within the human psyche—hard-headed economic rationality—often assumes itself to be superior to the more spiritual archetypes that are rooted in integrity.

'...[11] And now you say: Go tell your lord that Elijah is here. [12] As soon as I leave you, the spirit of YHWH will carry you somewhere I do not know, so when I tell Ahab and he cannot find you, he will kill me. I your servant have feared YHWH since I was a youth. [13] Was it not told to my lord what I did when Jezebel killed the prophets of YHWH, how I hid a hundred of YHWH's prophets, fifty in one cave and fifty in another, and fed them with bread and water? [14] And now you say: Go tell your lord that Elijah is here. He will kill me.'

Obadiah *argues*. This is a good sign, like Jacob wrestling with the angel, wrestling with God. Rabbi Zalman Schachter-Shalomi wrote about the need to have it out with God in a night vigil, to tell God of our rage, without which our faith cannot become real and we have no right to tell God of our love. Our greatest anger, says Reb Zalman, is that God made us without our consent.[11] The Zen teachers have said if we meet the Buddha we should kill him. They burned Buddha statues as firewood, responding to objections by saying 'bring me a piece of wood that isn't Buddha and I'll burn that instead'. There is nothing other than God, nothing that does not have Buddha-nature, nothing that is not Buddha-nature, because everything is its own nature. When we realize that, the trees become more tree-like and the pebbles become more pebble-like. The Living Jesus in the Gospel of Thomas said: 'Split a piece of wood, I am there. Lift a stone, and you will find me there.'[12]

But does Obadiah really see Elijah as a fully embodied human being? He fears the spirit of YHWH will carry him away, to a distant place or even somewhere that cannot be expressed in terms of place. It reminds me of people's reaction to the newly-enlightened Buddha, who was asked if he was a God (a *deva* or a *gandhabba* in Pali) or a nature spirit (*yakkha*). He was just someone who was awake, he replied truthfully. According to the *Dona Sutta*, the Buddha also refused to identify himself as human, because he had destroyed the 'fermentations' that would lead to a human rebirth, and, according to Thanissaro Bhikkhu, because 'an awakened person cannot be defined in any way at all.'[13] Obadiah expects Elijah to know that he hid and fed the prophets of YHWH, even though Ahab doesn't. Of course Elijah is a prophet, but at this point he symbolizes our true nature, our mind or consciousness being 'clear and knowing'. Our Buddha-nature knows our samsaric nature, but not *vice versa*. Fully embodied but undefinable, to have Buddha-nature is not to be less human, but to be fully human. A dog has Buddha-nature by being fully canine, which is why Zen Master Joshu was right to reply *mu* (no, or nothing) when asked if a dog had Buddha-nature.

Obadiah repeats his distrust of Ahab, complaining about Elijah's intention to send him back, and this is repeated, which is significant in itself. We look at the significance of repetition in the story of Elijah later. Obadiah states he has 'feared' YHWH since his youth, but he needs to take that next step of faith, to come face-to-face with YHWH, to realize his non-duality with YHWH.

[15] *Elijah said: 'As YHWH Sabaoth lives, before whom I stand, I will definitely show myself to him today.'* [16] *So Obadiah went to Ahab and told him, and Ahab went to meet Elijah.*

Elijah relents, is compassionate toward Obadiah, and assures him he won't disappear—the Buddha-nature won't abandon the seeker to samsara again, which is what Obadiah had feared. Whereas rebirth was once a passive consequence of karma, it has become an active decision rooted in *bodhicitta*. Elijah uses the phrase 'YHWH Sabaoth'—traditionally 'LORD of hosts' and paraphrased by Eugene Peterson as 'God-of-armies-of-angels'— and adds 'before whom I stand', as he did at the beginning of his story. He indicates to Obadiah that he, Elijah, is not an object of worship, but a soldier in the army of YHWH, a finger pointing to the moon.

Obadiah goes on his way, no longer clinging to the notion that he is having a vision of Elijah, not clinging to what feels like a blissful or supernatural experience, but going back to the marketplace, to use the Zen metaphor from the ox-herding pictures.[14] Obadiah's role in the story is at an end, but he has shown 'there are thousands of ways of being *almost* yourself.'[15] So he goes to Ahab, and Ahab goes to Elijah, but Ahab's spiritual search has been secondary to his self-cherishing, self-preservation, economic rationalism, keeping the animals alive. So it is Elijah who *shows himself* to Ahab. Even the most distant, most indirect glimpse of enlightenment is a moment of grace. We cannot find it by seeking, yet only seekers find it.

> [17] *When Ahab saw Elijah, he said to him: 'Is it you, you troubler of Israel?'* [18] *Elijah answered: 'I have not troubled Israel, but you and your father's house have, because you have forsaken the commandments of YHWH and followed the Baals.* [19] *Therefore, gather all Israel together now, and send them to me at Mount Carmel, and also send the four hundred and fifty prophets of Baal and the four hundred prophets of Asherah who eat at Jezebel's table.*

Ahab speaks first, as royal protocol would demand, but in doing so he shows himself oblivious to Elijah's *spiritual* rank. Isn't that the way with our materialist selves, which imagine hard-headed economic rationalism to outrank the life of the spirit? Ahab also seems oblivious to the meaning of Israel as one who *struggles* with God. How can one who struggles with God not be troubled by God? Elijah seems a bit defensive here, but he points out that Ahab and Israel have turned away from their true selves, that is, their non-dual non-selves, to the duality of self and Baal. This is something that comes from the top, from the hard-headed consciousness (or lack of consciousness) represented by Ahab, which sees itself as superior; hence the easy coexistence of Baal, who represents dualism, and Asherah, who represents materialism and the craving for material comfort and self-preservation.

When Elijah says they have 'forsaken the commandments', he points to the ethical character of the commandments, and to their role in the cultivation of mindfulness. There is a Jewish tradition that says each of the six hundred and thirteen commandments, *mitzvot*, is a way of coming closer to God, of developing what Muslims call *taqwa* (God-consciousness) and Buddhists call *sati* (mindfulness). However, the perennialist idea implies that all religious and spiritual traditions come from the same root, belong to a family tree with a single apical ancestor, with some arguing this apex is an ethical one. The search for common ground between religious and spiritual traditions is essential, but I don't think that common ground is to be found in ethics. Kierkegaard distinguished between the aesthetic, ethical and religious spheres of life, and to illustrate this he discussed Abraham's willingness to sacrifice his son (Isaac in the Bible, Ishmael in the Qur'an).[16] Abraham acted religiously, but he certainly didn't act ethically. We need to be consistent in rejecting the notion that religion is *founded* on ethics, including the notion that Buddhist practice is founded on *sila*. At best, this is a stage. At worst, it is an obstacle or even a dead end, as John Bunyan illustrated in *The Pilgrim's Progress*. Martin Luther is famous within Christianity for his emphasis on grace, but the grace-works tension is not a uniquely Christian one. I have already argued that the Golden Rule—often cited as the ethical foundation and common ground between religions—is about more than ethics, because unlike the so-called platinum rule it encompasses *anatta*. *Anatta* has profound ethical implications, but the fact they are *implications* means they are not at the *apex* of the family tree.

There is obvious hyperbole in Elijah's reference to '*all* Israel', but this shows it is a reference to those who struggle with God, who are unsure about following the non-dual path of being-itself, YHWH. As we shall see, there is a significance in the choice of Mount Carmel, and Elijah's successor Elisha also goes there on the first journey of his prophetic ministry.[17] The Hebrew word for prophets is *neviim*, and the word is used of the prophets of Baal and Asherah just as it is of Elijah; later in the story, we even encounter a reference to 'a lying spirit' being put in the mouths of the prophets by YHWH. In Jewish and Christian culture, the prophets of Baal are often called 'the priests of Baal', but that is not in the text.[18] The prophets of Baal and Asherah are both summoned, but the prophets of Asherah never appear, and the fact they don't appear is never even mentioned, though they *seem* to reappear later, as we shall see. Their decision to stay away from Mount Carmel is probably a good decision, given what later happens to the prophets of Baal.

There is more than a hint of misogyny in the representation of Jezebel in this story. She is the archetypal temptress, like Eve with the forbidden fruit and the daughters of Mara. Asherah is a Goddess, often regarded in the region as the consort of El or even of YHWH. Her name means 'the groves', which could be deliberate wordplay, not for the first or last time in the story of Elijah, and here she is a symbol of material comfort and complacency, like the *devas* of Buddhist cosmology. Elijah has tried to set up a three-way confrontation between duality, non-duality and materialism—all of which confront each other in all of us—but the materialists stay away. The dualists, the prophets of Baal, have the courage to turn up (which makes the outcome seem unfair), but their courage is a form of arrogance, and that makes them easier to defeat. The defeat of the prophets of Asherah takes much longer and requires what Buddhists call skillful means, which our text later calls a lying spirit in the mouth of Ahab's prophets. This raises uncomfortable questions, as God's approach to undermining Ahab suggests the end justifies the means. However, we are not looking at the prophets of Baal and Asherah as external to Elijah. They represent *kleshas*, afflicted states of mind, obscurations.

At the same time, they do not merely symbolize the struggles of an otherwise comfortable middle-class spirituality. Elijah displays a political edge when he refers to the 'prophets of Asherah that eat at Jezebel's table' in a time of famine. Compare their middle-class comfort to the prophets of YHWH, who have been hidden in a cave by Obadiah, fed only bread and water. Those who eat at Jezebel's table in a time of famine are the antithesis of those who live simply in a time of plenty, something people do when they are seeking true liberation, like the Buddha and other ascetics and yogins of his time. The material comfort of the prophets of Asherah highlights the dangers of spirituality being used in the service of power, and becoming thoroughly perverted as a result. This is by no means alien to the world religions, including Christianity and Buddhism. The philosopher Slavoj Žižek has compared Western Buddhism to Karl Marx's 'opium of the people', arguing it allows us 'to fully participate in capitalist dynamics while retaining the appearance of mental sanity'.[19] There is some truth in this. But Elijah's Buddhism is not a comfortable middle-class spirituality that eschews political analysis and involvement. His politics are the politics of *anatta*, not-self. *Anatta* has a political as well as a spiritual meaning, and these meanings cannot be separated. In Buddhist language, they are not two.

The *Kleshas* (1 Kings 18:20–40)

This passage juxtaposes an external deity, conceived dualistically, with YHWH the ground of being, who is *necessarily* nearer to us than our innermost being and therefore not to be shouted at or awakened through self-harm. It is a tantalizing glimpse of the gentle whisper, the still silence-sound in the next chapter. There is an emphasis on the name 'Israel', meaning those who struggle with God. To recognize God as nearer to us than our innermost being, not dualistically separate from us, requires a struggle, not *away* from our true nature like a fish going upstream in search of the ocean, but a paradoxical struggle to be still. The Tibetan Buddhist discipline of *salam*, paths and grounds, posits stages beyond the realization of non-duality, and I think this is because there is a pitfall in non-duality, namely the temptation to create a duality of non-duality and duality. If we are intellectually committed to non-duality, proud of our non-duality, identifying ourselves with it and contrasting it to other people's duality, then we haven't grasped non-duality at all, never mind realized it.

However, that doesn't mean we are not on the *path* to realizing non-duality. Here, God is revealed *through* the henotheism and the one-God-per-nation worldview of the time. Like the Buddha's teaching, it is not about overthrowing worldviews but leading people to enlightenment, a greater knowledge of the ground of being—also known as God and *sunyata* or emptiness—and a *oneness* with the ground of being, *using* the worldviews of the time and place, like reincarnation or henotheism, to accomplish this. Whether they are mistaken or non-mistaken doctrines is beside the point. Like karma, they are features of *how we experience*, as opposed to *anatta* which is ontological, a mark of existence, suchness, how things really are.

²⁰ *Ahab sent word to all the children of Israel, and gathered the prophets together at Mount Carmel.* ²¹ *Elijah came near to all the people and said: 'How long will you limp between two opinions? If YHWH is God, follow YHWH, but if Baal is God, follow Baal.' The people did not answer a word.*

The earlier phrase 'all Israel' is repeated as 'all the children of Israel'. Again, it seems like hyperbole, but it symbolizes all the different aspects of struggling with God, symbolized in turn by the different characters: the materialists like Ahab and the prophets of Asherah, Obadiah, Elijah himself, and the people who 'limp between two opinions'. The call comes from Ahab, from the head rather than the embodiment of not-self. This is the way it must be, hence the Buddhist principle of only teaching dharma when asked to teach dharma.

What is the significance of Mount Carmel? The book of Amos suggests Mount Carmel was seen as a place of refuge *from* God,[1] something this text invites the reader to re-evaluate as dualistic. It could be a sanctuary, a place of safety, and that might be why Elisha goes there later. The name seems to mean 'God's vineyard'. The book of Amos is dated earlier than the book of Kings, suggesting this idea of Mount Carmel was already known and understood. The fact of it being a high place and therefore sacred (like in Tibetan Buddhism and Bön today) would also have been understood. It is a place where different levels of consciousness encounter each other. George MacLeod, founder of the Iona Community, said Iona was a thin place, as though heaven and earth were separated by no more than a sheet of tissue paper. This is true, but not in the way you might think. You don't step off the ferry to the muted sounds of trumpets from heaven, but you are surrounded by the sacredness of the everyday, the ordinary, the mundane.

It is Elijah who comes near. We think we seek enlightenment, but it is enlightenment that seeks us. If that were not the case, there would be a seeker and a sought, a *subject* that is separate from being-itself and an *object* that is being-itself. But the ground of being is only ever a subject, what Martin Buber calls the eternal Thou.[2] Elijah comes near to *all* the people, as enlightenment comes near to all the different aspects of samsara and the whole journey from samsara to enlightenment. Jesus didn't say, 'I am the goal.' He said, 'I am the way.'[3] And Elijah still hasn't reached his destination. He doesn't yet realize that a duality of non-duality and duality is still duality. He's on the way, but he's not there yet. As this passage shows, however, even his superficial realization of non-duality is a powerful remover of hindrances to awakening, obscurations, known in Buddhism as the *kleshas*. Sometimes this word is translated 'defilements', which carries many of the same connotations as 'sin', but they are metaphorically understood as clouds in the sky. They do not eliminate the true nature; the blue sky has not ceased to exist, it has just been temporarily obscured. We can think in terms of eliminating or transforming the *kleshas*. Which is it? At this point in the text, the answer is unclear, but it becomes clear later (and it is not an either/or).

Elijah asks: 'How long will you limp between two opinions?' The New JPS Tanakh translation uses the verb 'hop' rather than 'limp'. 'Limping' implies injury, while 'hopping' can imply a lack of mindfulness, a forgetfulness of the fact we have two legs—represented by our conventional selves and our true self, which is not-self. The phrase 'between two opinions' does not convey the Hebrew metaphor, which means 'on the two boughs' or 'on unequal legs',[4] which makes sense of the hopping/ limping ambiguity. Elijah is not criticizing their inability to decide what they believe, which system of theology they agree with and which they disagree with. It is not about systems. It is not an intellectual question. It is an existential challenge. Elijah places an emphasis on *following* rather than 'believing' or even 'worshipping'. To use the language of Buddhist philosophy, the people's 'hopping' or 'limping' demonstrates the 'root affliction' and 'mental factor' of afflictive doubt, which is 'a two-pointedness of mind with respect to the...truths' and 'has the function of serving as a basis for non-engagement in virtues'.[5] Here, it is a matter of henotheistic *praxis*—which is the unity of theory and practice—rather than monotheistic doctrine. It is the beginning of a journey from henotheism to monotheism to non-duality, which can be represented as pantheism or panentheism, though both of these terms over-intellectualize it. But the people 'did not answer a word' because, despite Elijah's henotheism and his existential challenge, they *perceive* his call as abstract, theological, not rooted in experience. So he tries again.

> [22] *Then Elijah said to the people: 'I am the only prophet of YHWH left, but Baal's prophets are four hundred and fifty.* [23] *So let them give us two bulls, and let them choose one bull for themselves, cut it in pieces and lay it on the wood, but not light a fire under it. I will prepare the other bull and lay it on the wood, and not light a fire under it.* [24] *You call on the name of your God, and I will call on the name of YHWH, and the God that answers by fire, let that one be God.' All the people answered: 'It is well spoken.'*

Elijah seems to contradict Obadiah's earlier statement that he has saved a hundred prophets. He probably feels he's on his own, but this theme seems to run. Elijah keeps being presented with the fact that there are other prophets of YHWH, and keeps complaining he is the only one. By bringing this up, the text highlights the difference between experience and reality, between phenomenology and ontology. By the end of the story, he will have realized he is not the only one, and can happily pass on his mantle (literally) to Elisha.

The reference to bulls is a reference to the 'highest' form of sacrifice, as one bull could produce many offspring, and would be a significant indicator of wealth. The parable of the widow's mite in the New Testament[6] shows that the external value of the offering is not what matters, but the internal level of the commitment. Elijah is aware of this, and so is the author of the text, but Elijah needs the bulls as a teaching method, because the people cannot see what is in his heart. Elijah asks for the bulls to be donated (whether by Ahab or the prophets of Baal is not clear) because he has little or no material wealth. Like the Buddhist and Christian monastics, what he has is not his own, a practical exercise in realizing not-self.

Then there is the first reference to fire in the story of Elijah, and this is an important theme. At the time of writing, toward the end of the Babylonian exile or shortly after, fire as a symbol was associated with Zoroastrianism, and by extension the Persian empire and Cyrus the Great, who allowed the exiles to return to the land of Israel. It is a pro-Cyrus symbol, but not unambiguously, because in the next chapter we read that 'YHWH was not in the fire'.

Elijah allows the prophets of Baal to choose first, using skillful means to entice the ego, which assumes itself to be the alpha male, to have the right to rule, to enjoy the first spoils. Elijah does not make a show of power, he does not let the materialistic or dualistic ego feel threatened. He even couches the challenge in dualistic terms, because non-duality is not about challenging dualism as a doctrine, but about lived experience.

This time the people respond to Elijah, because the beginning of the dharma has been expressed concretely, not as an abstract philosophy. Similarly, many terms in the Bible and in Buddhist teachings (as well as the teachings of other religions) have their roots in something earthy, concrete, solid, not abstract. The abstraction comes later. They originate as everyday words that are used for what we might call a religious purpose, but later become *identified* more-or-less exclusively with the religious meaning, which *changes* the meaning. We have already seen this dynamic in the words 'sin', '*klesha*' and 'mercy'. Other examples include dharma (a supporting pole), gospel (good news from a messenger, specifically of a birth), baptize (dip, immerse, wash, clean), belief (Hebrew *aman*, from a piece of ground just firm enough for a tent peg, of great practical significance to a tribe of desert nomads), Islam (submit, something nomads train their camels to do), and so on.

> [25] *Elijah said to the prophets of Baal: 'Choose one bull for yourselves and prepare it first, because you are many. Then call on the name of your God, but do not light a fire.'* [26] *They took the bull that was given to them, they prepared it and called on the name of Baal from morning to noon, saying: 'O Baal, answer us.' But there was no voice and no answer. They danced in a limp way around the altar which was made.*

Elijah speaks to the prophets of Baal directly, upping the stakes just a little, but he softens this by observing they are many. It is interesting that he actually encourages them to call on the name of Baal, which in any other context would be a violation of the commandments. But this is not about *vinaya*, law or even ethics. It is about the heart of dharma, the natural law of the universe. The *preparation* of the bull is emphasized, both for the prophets of Baal and later for Elijah. The *lojong* mind-training slogans of Atisha begin: 'First, train in the preliminaries.' In Vajrayana Buddhism and Bön the *ngöndro* preliminary practices are emphasized as preparation for the realization of non-duality. But Elijah's preparation will be more extensive. When the text says the prophets of Baal dance in a 'limp' or 'hopping' way around the altar, it repeats the same word Elijah used of Israel earlier, with the same connotations. Their dualistic consciousness and practice do not prepare them for a realization of non-duality.

The prophets of Baal call 'from morning to noon', because they had daytime consciousness only. We shall see the significance of that shortly. They call out, but there is 'no voice and no answer'.

The word translated 'voice' is *qowl*, more commonly translated 'sound'. Throughout the story of Elijah, YHWH does not answer with a voice or a sound because YHWH is not concerned with establishing doctrines or revealing propositions. In this chapter YHWH answers by burning up delusions and obstacles, *kleshas*, and later (as we shall see) YHWH answers in 'a still silence-sound' (again, *qowl*), but this does not lead to a change in the *propositional content* of what Elijah hears from YHWH. The prophets of Baal receive no answer because they are shouting to something external, understood dualistically, and are therefore not in a position to *hear* the answer in the silence of their own being. We need to quieten ourselves, to practice a silence of the lips and a silence of the heart, if we are to hear a response from the one that is closer to us than our innermost being.

[27] *At noon, Elijah mocked them: 'Cry louder, for he is a God. Either he is musing, or is gone aside, or is on a journey, or maybe he is sleeping and must be awakened.'*

Elijah mocks them because they are in the land of Israel, and Baal is a foreign God. This is still henotheism, even if it looks like monotheism to modern eyes. But is Elijah going too far here? Taunting the ego might be dangerous. Perhaps, but the humor has two implications.

First, the concept of humor in the Bible[7] and in Western thought from the ancient Greeks until the European Enlightenment of the eighteenth century is essentially a superiority theory—to laugh is to laugh *at* someone, and to joke is to joke *at* someone's expense. This has been superseded by the incongruity theory pioneered by Enlightenment philosophers Francis Hutcheson and Immanuel Kant, and, to a lesser extent, by the Freudian 'release' theory, according to which we laugh because of the temporary lifting of a taboo.[8] To the writers and early readers of this text, it would have been understood in terms of superiority theory, though not as systematically as in Aristotle's teaching a couple of centuries later. Perhaps it is unsurprising that the ancient Greek philosophers did not regard laughter as particularly virtuous. This attitude was carried into early Christianity: John Chrysostom claimed Jesus never laughed,[9] and even today any interpretation of Jesus' teachings as humorous is likely to meet with resistance. The Buddha also comes across as very humorless. Buddhists may wince at George Mackay Brown's phrase 'bland as Buddha' (which he contrasts with the 'characters, surrealist folk' of the recent past),[10] but nobody will fail to see what he means. I don't for a moment believe the Buddha really was bland and humorless, but he certainly comes across that way in many of the Buddhist scriptures.

Second, and in contrast, there is a connection between humor and the spiritual path. To say humor represents incongruity provokes the question: what is incongruous with what? For the sociologist and theologian Peter Berger, it is the familiar, everyday world that is incongruous with the world as we believe it ought to be. The irrationality and tragicomedy of the world is incongruous with the well-ordered, predictable and essentially 'nice' world we believe we 'ought' to live in. This in turn suggests we have a consciousness of such a world, which, while it does not exactly prove the *existence* of such a world, nonetheless provides a 'signal of transcendence'.[11] Berger's work *A Rumor of Angels*[12] is modeled on Thomas Aquinas's 'five ways' of proving—scholastically—the existence of God. For Berger, what is relevant is that there are 'signals of transcendence' in the *social* world, in our *social* lives. They do not point to an objective God out there, or indeed to any objectively transcendent meaning, but they do point to such meaning existing in human consciousness, even in a world of industrialization and secularization. And one of Berger's five ways is the argument from humor, which has just been outlined.

It isn't until noon that Elijah mocks the prophets of Baal, and there is still a long way to go. The meaning of the Hebrew phrase translated 'he is musing, or is gone aside, or is on a journey' is unclear. Some translations use 'meditating' rather than 'musing', while 'gone aside' or 'on a journey' may even imply Baal has gone to the toilet. The phrase about 'sleeping' is clearer. Contrast this with the Buddha being awake, the Buddha-nature being the awakened nature, the nature of mind being 'clear and knowing'. The true YHWH, that which is, is awake within us all the time, which is why we can 'pray without ceasing', as the prayer of the heart continues to pray itself.

²⁸ They cried aloud and cut themselves after their manner with swords and lances, until the blood gushed out over them.

They cry even louder. Imagine the cacophony and the smell of sweat and blood. Delusion begets delusion, karma increases, samsara is not only a cycle but a self-perpetuating cycle. Having made a mistake, we often try to dig ourselves out, thus making the hole we are in deeper. This turns into self-harm, as suffering begets greater suffering in the *clinging* attempt to alleviate suffering. This shows the futility of self-harm as a means to realize not-self. If this body is not the self, then what is the point in harming it? But it took even the Buddha some time to realize this, to draw back from extreme asceticism and embrace (and later teach) the middle way between luxury and asceticism, which can also be an object of attachment. The reference to 'their manner'—also translated 'custom' (NRSV) and 'practice' (New JPS Tanakh)—highlights the need to transcend attachment to religious rituals and ceremonies. According to Theravada Buddhism, this is a prerequisite, and often the final prerequisite, to becoming a stream-enterer (*sotapanna*), one whose journey to nirvana (*nibbana* in Pali) has become irreversible. The realization of emptiness, which is being-itself or YHWH, does not come from observing religious rituals, though it does not come from avoiding religious rituals either, because aversion is another form of clinging.

> [29] *And so it continued. When midday was past, they prophesied until the time of the sacrificial offering, but there was no voice and no answer, nor any that regarded.*

The Hebrew text does not state when the sacrificial offering was, but there is a variant reading in the Septuagint that strongly suggests it was evening, the time of the *ma'ariv* prayer in modern Judaism or the *maghrib* prayer in Islam, and a significant time in the Jerusalem temple, the time of the sacrificial offerings. Seemingly, it was also a significant time for the prophets of Baal. Reb Zalman said: 'Dawn and dusk are basic times to pray, because then you have daytime and nighttime consciousness at the same time'.[13] As the high places are thin places, so these are thin times, when there is a oneness of calmness and activity. According to Shunryu Suzuki:

> We have been taught that there is no gap between nighttime and daytime, no gap between you and I. This means oneness. But we do not emphasize even oneness. If it is one, there is no need to emphasize one.[14]

Even though the prophets of Baal continue until dusk, the time of the oblation, when daytime and nighttime consciousness are present together, they have exhausted themselves. They thought they could achieve enlightenment through effort and by clinging, instead of waiting and being quiet, allowing grace to work inside them. They tried to find by seeking, but they were not really seekers. Many translations say they 'raved' or 'raved on', but the word is 'prophesied'. As we have already seen, clinging to religious practices is a hindrance to stream-entry, not a vehicle to enlightenment. Consequently, there was no voice (again, *qowl*), no answer, 'nor any that regarded', that is, nobody paid any attention.

30 Elijah said to all the people: 'Come near to me.' All the people came near to him. He repaired the altar of YHWH that had been thrown down.

There is an invitation—representing grace—from Elijah to the people to come near to him. Earlier, Elijah came near to the people, whereas here Elijah invites the people to come near to him, which they do. There are stages in realizing not-self and non-duality: from a *recognition of* the other, to an *interaction with* the other, to a *complete oneness* of self and other. This is also the structure of Vajrayana practices, beginning with a visualization of the *yidam* as separate from the practitioner, followed by a visualization of the *yidam* as entering the practitioner, culminating in an experience of the *yidam* as completely one with the practitioner.

But prior to those practices are the preliminary practices, the *ngöndro*. The first thing Elijah does is to repair, emphasizing restoration rather than creation, not trying to learn something new but *un*learning the obscurations that prevent us from seeing things as they are, as little children do. Repairing also implies *tikkun*, repairing or restoring the universe to its right state of oneness with God, of social justice on earth and the *shekhinah* being reunited with *Ein Sof* in heaven. As above, so below. The Hebrew text goes further than 'repair', using the word *wayrappe*, which means 'and he healed'. The altar represents our spiritual lives, which are in need of healing, having been 'thrown down' by materialistic and dualistic impulses. There is a danger of reification in using the word 'repair'—portraying our spiritual lives as an external object—but the altar is healed, our spiritual lives are healed, as the widow's son was healed earlier.

³¹ Elijah took twelve stones, the number of the tribes of the sons of Jacob, to whom the word of YHWH came saying: 'Israel will be your name.' ³² With the stones he built an altar in the name of YHWH, and made a trench around the altar, large enough to contain two measures of seed. ³³ He put the wood on the altar, cut the bull in pieces, and laid it on the wood. ³⁴ He said: 'Fill four jars with water, and pour it over the offering and the wood.'

There is an emphasis on the name Israel, a reminder that it means 'he struggles with God'. The text establishes a link between Jacob, 'to whom the word of YHWH came', and Elijah, to whom the word of YHWH has also come. There is what Sufis call a *silsilah*, a chain of transmission, as there is one between the Buddhist and the Buddha, between the genuine seeker and all who have found, all who have become awake.

The stones Elijah uses to build the altar represent *using what is there*. To be enlightened doesn't mean adopting the trappings of an exotic culture, so he doesn't buy polished stones from a hippy shop in Jerusalem, or India, or Tibet. He uses what is at hand, finding the resources for enlightenment in his own life, his own mind, his own experiences. Parker Palmer says our vocation or calling is not a loud external voice telling us to be what we are not, but a quiet internal voice inviting us to be more fully who we truly are.[15] Rabbi Zusya famously said: 'In the coming world, they will not ask me: "Why were you not Moses?" They will ask me: "Why were you not Zusya?"'[16] Often the thing that most hinders us in being truly ourselves is the temptation to compare ourselves to others, positively or negatively. In Buddhist teachings this is seen as a form of pride, which is one of the 'root afflictions' that are at the root of all the other *kleshas*.

Elijah digs a trench for the water, which comes later. He knows he has other afflicted states of mind that are not so easily externalized. On the face of it, pouring all that water over the altar seems like a massive waste in a time of drought. For Elijah, it was all-or-nothing, like the Buddha when he resolved to sit in the one spot until he was enlightened, or like the marathon monks of Mount Hiei who vow to kill themselves if they do not achieve their goal.[17] Elijah is willing to give up something precious, possibly the most precious thing in the circumstances, without asking if it is economically worthwhile. In the Gospels, Jesus emphasizes again and again that we need to give up everything—our whole lives—if we are to find the treasure in heaven, to sell everything we have in order to buy the pearl of great price.[18] The woman traditionally identified as Mary Magdalene breaks an expensive jar of perfume over Jesus' feet.[19] Again, this is not about the economy of finding enlightenment, but the willingness to accept it is worth all we have, and more. No wonder the Dalai Lama wept when someone asked him for the easiest, quickest and cheapest way to enlightenment.[20]

He said: 'Do it a second time'; and they did it a second time. And he said: 'Do it a third time'; and they did it a third time. 35 The water ran all round the altar, and he also filled the trench with water.

The second and third times the text says they do what Elijah asks, but the first time it doesn't. That's not the sort of omission that happens by accident in the Tanakh. It reflects the earlier healing of the widow's son, when Elijah stretched out three times to symbolize the personal, the impersonal and the interpersonal, which is ultimately a oneness with YHWH the ground of being. He stretched out for himself, not wanting to look like a fool or a fraud, a second time for the child, and a third for a non-dual transcendence, where there is no room for anything but God, an intimation of absolute *bodhicitta*. Here on the mountain, he asks for the trench to be filled for himself and his status as a prophet, not to mention his life, but the people's reaction is one of complacency. The second time is for himself and the people, for whom he has a real love, and the third is for the transcendent non-duality, YHWH, so the people realize something is happening. The water cuts off the altar, as the Red Sea and the Jordan cut off the Promised Land. There is no short cut. We need to cut through the *kleshas*, our afflictive states of mind, not take the short cut of pretending they are not there. A short cut would end up taking longer—more haste, less speed. To meditate with enlightenment as a *goal*, or with liberation as a *goal*, can be a hindrance to meditation, thereby frustrating the goal. We need to be fully present, *in* the present, even in the present moment.

> [36] *At the time of the sacrificial offering, Elijah the prophet came near and said: 'YHWH, God of Abraham, Isaac, and Israel, let it be known today that you are God in Israel, that I am your servant, and I have done all these things at your word. [37] Hear me, YHWH, hear me, so this people may know that you, YHWH, are God, for you have turned their hearts back.'*

Elijah is referred to as 'the prophet' for the first time in the Elijah story. He has come a long way, but his decision to pour water over the offering is what has 'upgraded' him to a prophet. In the New Testament, John the Baptist is identified with Elijah, and he also baptizes with water, whereas Jesus baptizes with *fire*.[21] Again, the text alludes to the time of the evening sacrificial offering, when there is both daytime and nighttime consciousness. Perhaps Elijah is mingling his prayer with that of the faithful in Jerusalem, in Judah. Practices such as prayer, meditation and fasting seem to be enhanced when we are conscious of other people doing the same practices. The times in the text don't add up—from the prophets of Baal finishing to Elijah praying seems almost instantaneous, whereas really it would take hours—but this highlights the symbolic nature of the story and its details.

Elijah addresses God as YHWH—the ground of being-itself—but also in the very personal and experiential way as 'God of Abraham, Isaac, and Israel', again emphasizing the struggle with God as the vocation of the people of Israel. The French philosopher Blaise Pascal used the phrase 'God of Abraham, God of Isaac, God of Jacob—not of the philosophers and scholars'.[22] Elijah brings a unity to the ontological and the experiential; the ground of being is *necessarily* beyond the dualism of the experiential and the ontological, but it is conceptually fragmented by philosophers and scholars. Rodger Kamenetz contrasts the 'scholarly intellectual way of reading Torah' that 'only breaks the text down into bits' with 'a deeper way of reading: a way that performs a *tikkun* on the text, and finds the light hidden in the text'.[23] I cannot claim my commentary achieves this, but that is its motivation, and I hope it will help or inspire others to do this for themselves.

Elijah wants it to be known that YHWH is God *in Israel*. This is henotheistic, but it is more specific, because he is addressing YHWH not only as the God of Judah but also the God *of* Israel, and the God *in* Israel. Yet again, he addresses YHWH as the God of those who struggle with God. There is a calm about Elijah, in contrast to the histrionics of the prophets of Baal, but still he wants a recognition of his *own* role. He is still like those who meditate for the sake of liberation or enlightenment; he is not yet at the stage of the great Sufi Rabia al-Basri, who longed to worship God solely from love of God, to the extent that she prayed to be burned in hell if she worshipped God from fear of hell, and excluded from paradise if she worshipped God in hope of paradise.

Yet Elijah's imperfect love of God is enough, like that of the publican who, we saw, asked for a juridical 'mercy' rather than a healing '*eleison*'. But then Elijah steps back from his request for recognition and asks that the people might know YHWH has 'turned their hearts back'. He puts the emphasis back on YHWH—non-dual being-itself, inside and out—and asks not for prestige among the people, but for the people to enter an I–Thou relationship with YHWH.[24] It is a non-dual experiential enlightenment where henotheism, monotheism, pantheism, panentheism and non-theism are all one: non-theism, that is, in Meister Eckhart's sense, who asked God to rid him of God, that is, of all his concepts of God, so he could experience the undivided reality that hides behind the word 'God'.

[38] *Then the fire of YHWH fell and consumed the offering, the wood, the stones, the dust, and even the water that was in the trench.* [39] *When all the people saw it, they fell on their faces and said: 'YHWH, YHWH is God; YHWH, YHWH is God.'* [40] *Elijah said to them: 'Take hold of the prophets of Baal. Do not let one of them escape.' So they took hold of them, and Elijah brought them down to the Kishon valley and killed them there.*

We have already seen that fire is a symbol associated with Zoroastrianism, and with Cyrus the Great who allowed the exiles to return from Babylon. It is also a symbol of the passionate, burning nature of enlightenment. In Buddhist circles, this is sometimes forgotten in favor of an emphasis on equanimity, but the very word 'enlightenment' reminds us that light has its origins in fire. In Rumi's *Mathnawi*, God tells Moses 'I want burning, burning,'[25] as opposed to the religious and theological correctness Moses had previously advocated. Fire is also a metaphor for the divine presence, as with the pillar of fire in the desert,[26] but we later learn that 'YHWH was not in the fire.'

The fire from heaven burns up the sacrificial bull, the wood, the stones of the altar, the dust, 'and even the water'. If taken literally, this phrase is strange. Completely incinerating large stones seems more impressive than turning liquid water into steam, so why 'and even'? Actually, a more literal meaning (reflected in the JPS Tanakh) is 'licked up', as an animal might lick up the very last drop of water, and it is this *intensity* and *completeness* that is conveyed by the words 'and even', which is why I have used them in my reworking of the JPS Tanakh. The words 'and even' are in several other translations, and they are what first pointed me to the need to understand this passage symbolically, and gave me a further nudge to draw on Buddhist resources to read the whole story of Elijah more psychologically. The transcendent non-duality, YHWH, burns up everything else, leaving only emptiness, the realization of which is *absolute bodhicitta*, which is paradoxically the ultimate fullness, encompassing and transcending *even relative bodhicitta*, the mind of compassion. So the water represents relative *bodhicitta*, which is licked up until there is nothing left, hence the words 'and even'.

What happens to the prophets of Baal is mass murder, which cannot and must not be justified with any theological gymnastics. Commentators and preachers who *try* to justify it should not be trusted to look after your children or pets. Kierkegaard told a story of a man who heard a preacher extolling Abraham's faith in being willing to sacrifice his son at God's command. The man was so inspired that he killed his own son on a sacrificial altar, and was arrested and imprisoned. The next Sunday, the same preacher lamented the breakdown in society that had led the man to do something so evil.[27]

In his novel *The Last Kabbalist of Lisbon*,[28] Richard Zimler comments on the Abraham story. One of his characters points out that Isaac's name means 'he laughed', and that this points us to the need to be sure the Torah is using metaphors, riddles even. According to this interpretation, Abraham was giving up a part of himself to create a space for God to enter. It reflects the idea of *tzimtzum* in Jewish mysticism, that God contracted, shrank, in order to make room for creation.

In this passage, it is the phrase 'and even the water' that points us to the need to be sure the Tanakh is using metaphors, riddles. Metaphorical does not mean less than literal; it means more than literal. The four hundred and fifty prophets of Baal symbolize Elijah's inner *kleshas*; they are obstacles to awakening in his own psyche. Even in announcing their deaths, the text calls them 'prophets' (*neviim*) *like Elijah*, showing they are one with Elijah. Specifically, they are *kleshas* relating to dualism, which are destroyed and transformed. How their destruction is a transformation is not yet clear—we need to be patient. The four hundred prophets of Asherah represent *kleshas* relating to self-preservation, or, more pertinently, preservation of the self, and they are only destroyed and transformed at the end of the Elijah story.

The people's response is not one of non-duality, but it is a step. They repeat the call that YHWH is God. This is not a theological statement but an existential conviction. It is expressed with the Hebrew word *hu*, so the phrase 'YHWH, YHWH is God' can also be translated 'YHWH, He is God', with an emphasis on the capitalized 'He'. I find it impossible to express the meaning of this adequately. It is not the same as the lower-case masculine 'he', but it is not gender-neutral either. The Sufis often say *la illaha illa hu*—there is no God but He—and *Allah Hu*—God is. It is apophatic, a finger pointing to the moon. God is not masculine, or feminine, or gender-neutral. God *is*. YHWH *is*. There is a rawness in the people's confession, but it still points to the ground of being. Indeed, it is *because* of that rawness that it points to the ground of being. 'God of Abraham, God of Isaac, God of Jacob—not of the philosophers and scholars.'

There is an urgency about the moment. The *kleshas* need to be held, dealt with decisively, destroyed quickly, or else they might escape and *rebuild*, but not *heal*, the entire dualistic ego system. However, Mount Carmel is a place of sanctuary, even for the *kleshas*, and they can only be destroyed in accordance with truth and integrity. This is not a time for skillful means. So they go to the Kishon valley, 'Kishon' meaning 'slaughter'. It is where Yael killed Sisera, when heavy rain and mud slowed the chariots of the enemy, when Barak was determined not to let a single one escape, and indeed the Kishon swept them away.[29] Elijah is following in the path of previous bodhisattvas before him. Sisera was a great general—equivalent to the most hard-to-uproot *kleshas*—and according to the Talmud, Jael used the skillful means of having sex with him seven times, in order to exhaust him before killing him with a tent peg.[30] Remember that the Hebrew *aman*, meaning belief or faith, derives from a piece of ground just firm enough for a tent peg, so the *klesha* was uprooted with the power of faith. This is not belief in propositions or creeds, but the spiritual nomad recognizing a *need* for shelter and resolving to find the way home, to pitch one's spiritual tent in the field of *experiential* oneness with YHWH. In Buddhism, this tent would be called a refuge. Also in the Talmud, Sisera's descendants were said to have become teachers of the young in Jerusalem,[31] so uprooting the *kleshas* doesn't merely destroy them, but turns them to positive states of mind, realization of the dharma, like the poisoned tree in Vajrayana Buddhism that is used to make medicine.

The Liminal Stage (1 Kings 18:41–19:9a)

The anthropologist Arnold van Gennep coined the idea of the liminal stage in his 1909 book *The Rites of Passage* (*Les Rites de Passage*). In many rituals there is a separation stage where participants experience a disconnect from their former life and community, and a reintegration stage where they re-enter the same community but with a different status, such as a baptized person, a *hajji* or a Buddhist monk. The liminal stage is in between, when the participant is no longer one thing but not yet the other. In a Theravada Buddhist ordination ceremony, the ordinand is given the name 'Naga' for the duration of the ceremony, indicating they have left their former name behind but not yet been conferred an ordination name. In Christian baptism, when it is by immersion, there is a very brief moment when the person is under the water, neither baptized nor unbaptized. Like this one, some liminal stages are very short, while others can last for years.

This part of the story of Elijah is a liminal stage for him. He has uprooted the *kleshas* symbolized by the prophets of Baal; he has even been called Elijah the Prophet, but he is not yet the finished article. He will go on a solitary journey, and encounter YHWH in a more direct way than ever before. The liminal stage is a dangerous stage. If you drown in the baptistry, do you die as a baptized person or an unbaptized person? Does a Theravada ordinand who doesn't make it through the ceremony remain a Naga, which means snake? If you've left childhood behind but not entered adulthood, what are you? The Zen masters say that before enlightenment mountains are mountains and rivers are rivers, during enlightenment—the liminal stage—mountains are not mountains and rivers are not rivers, and after enlightenment mountains are mountains and rivers are rivers. No wonder

Elijah has massive mood swings in his liminal stage, fearing for his life one moment, wishing he might die the next. But first, as is often the case at the separation stage, he has some loose ends to tie up.

[41] Elijah said to Ahab: 'Go up, eat and drink, because there is a sound of abundant rain.'

Elijah's instruction to Ahab seems like a non sequitur: why should it follow from the sound of rain that Ahab should eat and drink? This, and his almost friendly tone, indicates Elijah doesn't want to destroy Ahab, as the enlightened mind doesn't want to destroy the illusory self that Ahab represents, but transform it into a cause of enlightenment, like in Vajrayana Buddhism where *kleshas* are symbolized by poisons that can be transformed into medicines. Ahab is traumatized, and Elijah wants to heal him. Even though they are on top of a mountain, Elijah tells Ahab to go *up*, to *ascend*—the Hebrew is explicit on this—encouraging him to move on to something higher. There is the sound of rain before the rain itself, as there is the word of YHWH before YHWH passes by in the next chapter, symbolic (and perhaps more than symbolic) of divine emanation, the more 'accessible' emanations drawing us 'upward'. It is the same with enlightenment, which is why the ten ox-herding pictures in Zen Buddhism don't *end* with enlightenment. It is not an end, but a new beginning, going from one beginning to another, as Brother Roger of Taizé used to say.[1] In Ahab's case, he doesn't continue, but it is a new beginning for Israel, a new phase of struggling with God.

[42] So Ahab went up to eat and drink. Elijah went up to the top of Mount Carmel, he bowed himself down upon the earth, and put his face between his knees.

Ahab takes Elijah's advice, though it seems that any advice not relating to self-preservation is less welcome. Elijah goes to the top of the mountain, returning to the sanctuary, and bows with his face between his knees. This is a posture of humility as well as a deep drawing in, bringing together our spirit within ourselves. Alphonse and Rachel Goettmann identify it with the yoga position 'folded leaf' and with the *sajdah* in Muslim prayer.[2] It is not a common meditation posture in Buddhist meditation, but all postures have a significance. Kneeling in meditation can help transcend the sometimes-perceived distinction between meditation and prayer—if we understand this then we understand both meditation and prayer more deeply, more fully, than if we contrast them. Like Alyosha in *The Brothers Karamazov*, Elijah bows down and kisses the earth. Alyosha and Elijah demonstrate compassion for the earth, which has been damaged by a spiritual drought, a lack of concern, materialistic values.

[43] *Elijah said to his servant: 'Go up now, and look towards the sea.' He went up and looked, and said: 'There is nothing.' Elijah said: 'Go again seven times.'*

There is no previous reference to Elijah having a servant. There is a sense of expectation, a hope for something, hence the repetition of the words 'Go up' which were used earlier. This sense of expectation is a servant of the enlightened mind, *bodhicitta*, and not its master. It may be a hope for something material—rain, better harvests, increased prosperity—but still this is a servant and not a master for Elijah. He has to go deep, to the seventh level. The number seven is often seen as a perfect number, and there is no shortage of speculation as to why this might be. Biblical numerology can be a minefield, but it can also be an opportunity for a speculative, imaginative, playful approach to the text, following the principle this book began with, that the more interpretations that increase our love of the becoming possible of the impossible, and that help to reconcile our spiritual traditions, the better. In Theravada Buddhism, it is said the stream-enterer (*sotapanna*) will be reborn a maximum of seven more times before becoming an *arahant*, one who has attained *nibbana* (*nirvana* in Sanskrit). Insight meditation is sometimes characterized as the mind watching the mind, but there is another level where the mind watches the mind that watches the mind, and so on. It is said that very few people, if any, can get beyond the sixth level of this process, so for Elijah to go as deep as the seventh level would mean he is not doing it by his own individual power, but by transcending his individuality, realizing not-self.

[44] *The seventh time he said: 'A cloud is rising out of the sea, as small as a man's hand.' Elijah said: 'Go up and tell Ahab to make his chariot ready and get himself down, so that the rain will not stop him.'*

This is a very subtle sign—the moment of enlightenment comes like the tiniest of signs, a cloud no bigger than a person's hand, and this contains everything. This small amount is enough to drench everything. In kabbalah even the soles of God's feet are so glorious as to be the *shekhinah*, which a human being cannot look upon and live, that is, it burns up our egos entirely. Ahab would not be able to cope, so Elijah gives him this warning.

[45] *The heavens were soon black with clouds and wind, and there was heavy rain. Ahab rode to Jezreel.* [46] *The hand of YHWH was on Elijah, who tied his cloak around his waist and ran before Ahab to the entrance of Jezreel.*

But Elijah can cope, on foot. The enlightened mind can handle the sheer beauty of enlightenment in a way that the dual or materialistic mind cannot, because it is non-dual, it is one with the rain, 'one with the laws of causation',[3] one with the dharma. The dharma comes to be written on our hearts, not on tablets of stone, not as propositions in the form 'this, not that'. Some translations of the New Testament into Asian languages render the Greek word *logos* as *dharma* or *dhamma*: 'In the beginning was the dharma, and the dharma was with God, and the dharma was God.' At first it was alone, then it was in company, and ultimately it was non-dual.

Heaven and sky are also non-dual, the same word in Hebrew, which I have rendered as 'the heavens'. We can't say one is sacred and one secular. As a child I once asked how far down does the sky come, and was told it came all the way down to the ground.

19 Ahab told Jezebel all that Elijah had done, and how the prophets were all killed with the sword. [2] *Jezebel then sent a messenger to Elijah, saying: 'So let the Gods do to me, and more also, if I do not make your life like their lives by this time tomorrow.'*

Ahab seemingly expects Jezebel to be impressed with what Elijah has done. On the face of it, Ahab's dualism is more opposed to non-duality than Jezebel's materialism. But dualism can see the possibilities in non-duality, because the two confront each other and debate with one another. In a way, they try to help each other, like Tibetan monks in debate. Materialism, on the other hand, thrives on indifference. In Coleman Barks's translation of Rumi, Jesus flees from such indifference, even though he has no need to be afraid of anyone.[4] Nicholson's more literal translation of Rumi refers to the 'fool' and his 'folly',[5] rather than indifference, but the fool who says in his heart 'there is no God'[6] is the same as Caputo's 'loveless lout' who is indifferent to everything except economic gain (and this has nothing to do with an intellectual position on synthetic propositions regarding the existence or non-existence of God).

Jezebel says 'the Gods'. The Hebrew is *Elohim*, which is plural, but it is frequently translated as 'God', even though the singular *Eloah* was available to the Biblical writers and indeed is sometimes used. So there is some theological bias in translating it as 'God' in some places and 'Gods' in others.[7] Even on a linguistic level, however, this is not straightforward, because the noun *Elohim* is sometimes written with a singular verb and sometimes (as here) with a plural verb, but the fact remains that *Elohim* is always a plural noun. In the ancient world it was often understood that the singular 'God' could be used interchangeably with the plural 'Gods'. We find this in Plato, and it can still be seen in Hinduism, which is both polytheistic and monotheistic, the one formless God Brahman existing in many avatars, manifestations or Gods. In the story of Elijah, and the Tanakh as a whole, the singular and plural concepts of God, or rather experiences of God, are genuinely juxtaposed, but in a rather confusing way. This suggests a possible Yahwist/Elohist tension in the redaction of the text, but it also reminds us of the principle that statements about God must be apophatic[8]—God is not this, God is not that— and indeed of the Buddha's noble silence in response to certain questions. Many Buddhist scholars and teachers have attempted to interpret this silence, to say 'what the Buddha meant by his silence was...', but none of them overcomes the objection that if the Buddha really meant that then he could have said it, and he didn't.

Presumably Jezebel doesn't understand the value of silence. If she does, why does she send a messenger to warn Elijah? She has given him a twenty-four hour start. Does she want him to suffer rather than die? I don't think so. On the face of it, she wants revenge, but we have seen that materialism thrives on indifference, and she knows there is something in him that can never die. The *kleshas* have not simply been 'killed with the sword'—they have been annihilated and transformed into the prerequisites of the *sotapanna*, the stream-enterer, whose flow to the sea of liberation is irreversible. Like King Canute commanding the sea to stop before his throne, Jezebel is overreaching, and knows she is overreaching. The materialist mind is overreaching, and knows it is overreaching. It knows its limitations, but turns a blind eye to them, convincing itself it is the *hard head*, in terms both of realism and authority.

> ³ *So Elijah fled for his life. He went to Beer-sheba which belongs to Judah, and left his servant there.* ⁴ *He then went a day's journey into the wilderness, alone, and sat under a broom tree. He requested for himself that he might die, and said: 'It is enough. Now, YHWH, take away my life, for I am no better than my fathers.'*

The text says he 'fled for his life', but the Hebrew *napsaw* can mean heart, mind, or soul (as in the story of the widow of Zarephath's son), as well as life. The Buddhist principle of *anatta*, not-self, is sometimes taken to be a dogmatic statement that there is no such thing as the self, and in this spirit is sometimes translated 'no self' and even 'no soul'. But it is really a challenge. Is this body the self? Is this mind the self? This consciousness or that emotion? Where is the self? Point it out to me! It is like Thomas Aquinas's version of apophatic theology, the *via negativa*, in which the more things we can say God is *not*, the closer we come to what God *is*. Every time we meditate we discover something new about what meditation is *not*. The 'soul', in Elijah's life or your life, is the empty space in which body, mind, consciousness, emotion and many other things intersect. The 'heart' does not refer to the organ inside the body, but to this center, this empty space. There is no such 'thing' as the self or the soul because it is not a thing. It is more like a gravitational pull of things to each other, or to use a different metaphor, it is a construction project rather than a thing that has been constructed.

There is more than a hint of self-preservation in Elijah's actions, not least as he goes to the southern kingdom of Judah, but *he leaves his servant there*. His desire for self-preservation is no longer his servant. He is briefly mastered by it, then he swings to the opposite extreme and gets rid of it altogether. He goes into the wilderness, representing a dark night of the soul. Jesus voluntarily went to the wilderness to be tempted, and Gautama voluntarily experienced extreme asceticism before his enlightenment and Buddhahood.

Elijah is not yet at that stage. He seems to be going backward, like someone walking the labyrinth who appears to be getting further from the center but in reality is getting closer. It is only after we have walked the path that it looks in any sense orderly. Beforehand, it seems chaotic. Because he has got rid of his servant, Elijah asks YHWH to take away his life; again, the Hebrew word is *napsaw*. His comment comparing himself to his fathers — either biological ancestors or social fathers from his nomadic encampment — indicates a loss of faith in the possibility of breaking through from the bodhisattva motivation to the stage of a stream-enterer or Buddha. He is like the bodhisattva Chenrezig momentarily being overwhelmed by the thought of all the suffering in the world and shattering into many pieces, before being helped by Amitabha Buddha. Elijah comments 'it is enough'. He feels he has striven for enlightenment — 'only seekers find it' — but not got there. This apparent hopelessness is a crucially important stage, when the seeker is open to the moment of grace — it 'can never be found *by* seeking'.

⁵ He lay down and slept under a broom tree, and an angel touched him and said: 'Rise and eat.' ⁶ He looked, and there at his head was a cake baked on hot stones and a jug of water. He ate and drank and lay down again. ⁷ The angel of YHWH came a second time, and touched him and said: 'Rise and eat, because the journey is too great for you.' ⁸ He arose, and ate and drank…

He falls asleep, there is a sense of tiredness. Sometimes when we 'have it out with God' there is a sense of tiredness remaining, rather than anger. An angel appears. The Hebrew word translated 'angel' is *malak*, the same word translated earlier as 'messenger'. It looks like a deliberate juxtaposition, which implies it has some significance. It has been observed that the one sent by Jezebel is a messenger of death, while the one sent by YHWH is a messenger of life.[9] So death is the message of materialism, while life is the message of the ground of being, of non-dual being-itself. I think there is something in this, but taken alone I find it too neat, too arbitrary, too dualistic, in the sense of a dualism of duality and non-duality.

There is a Zen *koan* in which two students argue about something, perhaps the meaning of emptiness or compassion. Master Nansen grabs a cat, holds a sword over it and says: 'If either of you can say a good word, I will not chop this cat in two.' Nobody says a good word, so Nansen carries out his threat. Later, Master Joshu comes back from a journey. When Nansen tells him the story, Joshu puts his shoes on his head and walks out of the room backward. 'If you had been there,' Nansen tells him, 'you would have saved the cat.' Kōun Yamada Roshi comments on this *koan*:

> Nansen's sword kills everything, and Jōshū gives everything life. They represent the two sides of Zen activity. One side, represented by Nansen, extinguishes or cuts off delusions which arise fundamentally from opposing subject and object. The significance of this is to cut off all evil. There is a Zen saying, 'There is not even a grain of dust in the

essential world.' ...The other side of Zen activity is to give life to everything. Jōshū presents this side uniquely by his extraordinary action. Its significance is to practice all good. There is a Zen saying, 'Nothing remains outside the Buddha's Dharma.' In order to promote...spiritual advancement, both are indispensable.[10]

So the messenger of death and the angel of life are both indispensable, but we still have the question: why a *malak*? I think the key to this can be found in Kabbalah, where an angel is understood as the embodiment of a task. It is not that the angel *performs* a task, but that the angel *is* a task. This is supported by the immediate disappearance from the narrative of both *malakim*. Also, it is a feature of the Elohist narrative that communication between God and humans occurs through the medium of *malakim*. Once more, this touches on the difference — which is only gradually erased in the labyrinth-like journey to non-duality — between experience and ontology.

The angel touches him, as the angel touched Jacob on the hip before giving him the name Israel, meaning he struggles with God. As Gautama hadn't looked after himself neither had Elijah, so his immediate need for sleep and food are what is provided. He sleeps, he is able to rest and recuperate, and to dream. Maybe this is all a dream sequence, and the strength Elijah gets (which, as we shall see, is a considerable strength) is a *spiritual* strength from the dream. In other words, the dream gives him the inspiration to continue his work. In working on this commentary, I have been inspired by dreams on more than one occasion. There is nothing intrinsically mystical about this; there are scientific breakthroughs that have been inspired by dreams, most famously Kekulé's discovery of the structure of the benzine molecule.

Elijah is *awakened* — and Buddha means one who is awakened — by the angel. The cake is baked on hot stones. Before reaching this passage, I had a dream about cooking on hot volcanic stones. In both cases, there is a very earthy symbolism. Although an angel is present, the scene is about the stuff of normal everyday life, which is sacralized and transformed into the raw material for enlightenment. He eats and drinks and sleeps again, but there seems to be a different quality to his sleep this time. It is no longer the sleep of exhaustion, of feeling dispirited and of wanting to give up.

The angel comes a second time, after Elijah has slept a second time, and tells him to eat a second time. Both times the angel tells him to eat, both times he eats *and drinks*. Again the angel touches him, and this time he doesn't go back to sleep. Jacob was touched once, Elijah twice. Jacob was injured, Elijah was healed. The angel makes reference to the journey ahead, as though Elijah is aware of this and it needs no explanation. There is an element of freedom *from* choice here, characteristic of a certain level of realization, or enlightenment. Having a sense of self-preservation *as his servant* was a middle way between having it as master and not having it at all, but then he swung from one extreme to the other, and now he has found a new and better middle way—not just a compromise but something that transcends both extremes and even the earlier middle way. He hasn't realized non-duality yet, but he begins to realize not-self. The angel feeds him twice, allows him to sleep twice, wakes him twice, and touches him twice, because you don't realize non-duality by destroying one side. You need to look after both sides, and eliminate the division by transcending it. Marco Pallis points out that non-duality excludes all monistic explanations. This is philosophically rigorous. The dualism of mind and body, for example, is not transcended by saying what appears to be mind is really body, or what appears to be body is really mind. Non-duality means they are equally real, equally important, and ultimately of the same substance.

...and went in the strength of that meal for forty days and forty nights to Horeb the mountain of God. [9] There he came to a cave, and stayed there for the night.

As we saw earlier, after the Buddha was worn out by asceticism and realized its futility, he was given a bowl of rice and milk which gave him the strength to sit under the tree for as long as it took. Elijah has also been given the strength for his next push. It is not a final push to enlightenment as it was for the Buddha, but he is able to go in the strength of the angel's food for forty days, and this marks a significant change in Elijah. Rather than *striving* like a fish swimming upstream in search of the ocean, assuming enlightenment must require hard work, he begins to relax like a fish swimming downstream toward the ocean.

Forty days and nights is a common timeframe in the Bible. It was the duration of Noah's flood, and the time the Israelite spies spent in Canaan.[11] Goliath challenged the Israelites for forty days,[12] Moses spent forty days and forty nights on Mount Sinai on three occasions.[13] In the New Testament, Jesus spent forty days in the desert, and there were forty days between his resurrection and ascension.[14] If there is a significance to the number forty it is unclear what it might be, but again it allows us to experiment with some playful numerology. In Kabbalah, there are ten *sefirot* (emanations of God) in each of the four worlds (of action, knowledge, feeling, and spirit[15]), but *keter* (the crown) in a lower world is the same as *malkhut* (the *shekhinah*, the kingdom, or the soles of the feet) in the next one up, and this makes thirty-seven *sefirot*. The sefirot are all emanations of *Ein Sof* (Without End—utterly beyond any attempts to impose limitations of language or definition), who is an emanation of *Ein Ein Sof* (Without *Ein Sof*, beyond even those non-limits, beyond even any idea of beyond, to use the Sufi phrase), who in turn is an emanation of emptiness. This adds up to forty.

But whatever the significance of the number forty, the device puts Elijah in the company of other prophets and bodhisattvas, like the Buddha. He goes to 'Horeb the mountain of God', also known as Mount Sinai, as Moses did before. The story is clearly moving toward an enlightenment event—not a once-for-all enlightenment like the Buddha's, but one that is more consistent with representations of enlightenment in the Zen teachings, where enlightenment is a stimulus to further practice.

He comes to a cave, symbolic of focusing inwardly and also of re-entering the womb, which in turn is symbolic of divine mercy (*rahem*). Again he sleeps; he is following the middle way now.

Not in the Fire (1 Kings 19:9b–21)

And the word of YHWH came to him and said to him: 'What are you doing here Elijah?' [10] He said: 'I have been very jealous for YHWH the God of hosts, for the children of Israel have forsaken your covenant, thrown down your altars, and killed your prophets with the sword. I am the only one left, and they are trying to take away my life.'

The *word* of YHWH comes to Elijah, and again it seems somehow distinct from YHWH, at least in Elijah's still limited experience. There seems to be a hint of emanation here, where the word of YHWH is an emanation of YHWH, as the *sefirot* are emanations of *Ein Sof*, and ultimately of emptiness. For Elijah it is as though the different stages of awakening are emanations of enlightenment, an unfolding of enlightenment, though ultimately there is only one enlightenment. The question 'What are you doing here?' seems strange—surely he is where he is meant to be. It is like a *koan*, one that any one of us could ask ourselves at any time.

Elijah responds like a jealous lover. His complaint is like Jeremiah's—'you seduced me and I was seduced'[1]—but it is easy to feel entitled to some sort of recompense when we give up something in order to pursue a spiritual calling. It might even be a phase we need to go through. Although his reference to 'covenant' is still henotheistic—God in/of Israel—Elijah doesn't worry about 'theological correctness' here, nor does he question whether his claim to be the only prophet of YHWH left is even true. Furthermore, having recently (forty days before) asked that he might be allowed to die, he now complains they are trying to take away his life. His journey to enlightenment is a labyrinth rather than a straight line; he has had a glimpse of enlightenment, made one or two breakthroughs, and realizes the road to enlightenment has only just begun. His mini-*kenshos* are beginnings, not endings. That we go from one beginning to another can be a source of joy and hope, but it can also feel overwhelming. We want to get to the destination, we want to reach the goal, but we need to be fully present with the path. In that way the path is the goal and the goal is the path. When I did the Camino, one priest told a group of pilgrims about the need to fully experience the path itself, and not be so fixated on the destination as to miss the lessons of the actual Camino. So there is no contradiction between saying there is one enlightenment, yet his mini-*kenshos* are only beginnings.

[11] *He said: 'Go outside and stand on the mountain before YHWH.' And YHWH passed by, and a great and strong wind tore the mountains apart and broke the rocks in pieces before YHWH, but YHWH was not in the wind; and after the wind an earthquake, but YHWH was not in the earthquake;* [12] *and after the earthquake a fire, but YHWH was not in the fire; and after the fire a still silence-sound.* [13] *When Elijah heard it, he wrapped his face in his mantle and went out and stood in the entrance of the cave. A voice came to him and said: 'What are you doing here, Elijah?'*

But now, almost out of nowhere, comes the spiritual or psychological high point of the Elijah story. There is an apophatic element here: YHWH was *not* in the wind, *not* in the earthquake, *not* in the fire, but the text doesn't actually say where YHWH *was*. It seems to *imply* that YHWH was in the 'still silence-sound', but it doesn't say so directly.

'And YHWH passed by.' The concept of being-itself passing by as though having previously been in one place and in transit to somewhere else doesn't make sense if we read it objectively, so this must be phenomenological, a subjective experiential account of this moment in Elijah's journey toward enlightenment. The wind 'tore the mountains apart, and broke the rocks in pieces'—

hyperbole if taken literally, but isn't this like the experience we occasionally get in meditation, when everything we have known seems to be blown away and smashed to pieces—'but YHWH was not in the wind'—as when we regain our normal everyday consciousness and realize we did not just experience a sudden enlightenment after all? It is the same with the experience of the earthquake, those meditation experiences that shake us up and overturn our views of self and of the world. Those views really are illusory, but that is not what this is about, for 'YHWH was not in the earthquake'.

The fire burns up everything about us, what we thought we knew—'but YHWH was not in the fire'. The theme, the symbol of fire in the story of Elijah has already been mentioned, particularly in connection with Zoroastrianism, and as also noted earlier there is a striking contrast between the fire falling from heaven onto the altar at Mount Carmel and the insistence here that 'YHWH was not in the fire'.

And then there is the heart-stopping moment when the text says 'and after the fire a still silence-sound'. Traditionally this is rendered 'a still small voice', a beautiful phrase but one that has the effect of anthropomorphizing God, as does 'a gentle whisper'. The NRSV reads 'a sound of sheer silence' and more literally it reads 'a still silence-sound', both of which have the opposite effect. It may not quite be the sound of emptiness, but it is an intimation of it, the sound of one hand clapping, an invitation to Elijah to enter into a *direct experience* of emptiness. This is not something that can be understood—whether through the *sefirot* of Kabbalah or the inferential cognizer of Gelug philosophy.[2] As Thich Nhat Hanh says of the Holy Spirit, it can only be experienced.[3] Again, in meditation this is what we need to listen to—not the dramatic insights that are symbolized by the wind, earthquake and fire, but this gentle clarity, that stillness of the mind. The prophets of Baal couldn't hear it because they were shouting to something external. It is only when we quieten ourselves and pause our inner dialogue, practicing what Mother Teresa called a silence of the lips and a silence of the heart,[4] that we can hear the response.

Elijah recognizes this. Indeed, he hasn't even bothered to leave the cave for the wind, earthquake or fire. He has observed these phenomena as they arise in his mind, but he has not identified with them, nor has he identified them with ultimate reality. He covers his face, for no-one can see the *shekhinah* and live—and he does so with the mantle, which is mentioned here for the first time in the story. It is the symbol of his prophetic power and status, and it may be more than a symbol. Although YHWH was not in the fire, it is this emptiness that can burn us up, burn up the ego, which we confuse with life itself. Even with his level of realization, he is not ready for that, so he takes refuge in a symbol, as we often take refuge in religious rituals and ceremonies to protect ourselves from the direct experience of non-duality and emptiness. But these rituals and symbols are not necessarily to be avoided. As was said earlier, the *avoidance* of religious rituals can be another form of clinging.

The voice asks him the same question the word of YHWH asked him earlier. Before enlightenment mountains are mountains and rivers are rivers, during enlightenment mountains are not mountains and rivers are not rivers, after enlightenment mountains are mountains and rivers are rivers. This doesn't imply regression to a pre-enlightenment state, but nor is enlightenment the knowledge of a new proposition or the receipt of a new revelation. It is a *clarity*, about the things we have always had with us and in us.

[14] *He said: 'I have been very jealous for YHWH the God of hosts, for the children of Israel have forsaken your covenant, thrown down your altars, and killed your prophets with the sword. I am the only one left, and they are trying to take away my life.'*

Elijah repeats exactly what he said earlier. Is this because he doesn't get it? He seems to have missed something. The first question came from the *word* of YHWH, and this one comes from YHWH. Does Elijah think they are two? Or is he answering the question in a different way, recognizing the implication of the question—that enlightenment is not the receipt of new propositional knowledge, that mountains are mountains and rivers are rivers? There is a *koan* in which Joshu asks a question and gets a raised fist in reply, which he rejects as shallow. The next day he asks the same question to the same monk and gets the same reply, which he accepts as evidence of enlightenment. Is Elijah giving the right answer in *dokusan*, even though he is using the same words that were the wrong answer shortly before?

> [15] *YHWH said to him: 'Go, return on your way to the wilderness of Damascus, and when you come you will anoint Hazael to be king over Aram,* [16] *and Jehu the son of Nimshi you will anoint to be king over Israel, and Elisha the son of Shaphat of Abel-meholah you will anoint to be prophet in your place.* [17] *The one who escapes from the sword of Hazael, Jehu will kill, and the one who escapes from the sword of Jehu, Elisha will kill…'*

Elijah is sent back again, further than the journey he has just made. There is no need to cling to his experience of enlightenment by staying there; indeed, that would be counterproductive. The anointing of Hazael as king of Aram, outside the land of Israel, indicates a move from henotheism to monotheism, henotheism being more dualistic, monotheism *recognizing* a non-duality, at least as a potential (which is what emptiness is). In other words, non-duality is apophatic—God is *not* separate from *this*, God is *not* separate from *that*.[5] It is a process, a path, a way; not a doctrine, a notion, or a goal. When God alone exists, when God is being-itself, even panentheism and pantheism don't make *experiential* sense, still less the *analytical* distinction between them.

The rest of the Elijah story emphasizes the relations between Israel and Aram—including the ownership of Ramoth Gilead, where Elijah came from. It is not until the Elisha story that Hazael and Jehu become kings. There is an interesting juxtaposition of kings and prophets in these verses, and the entire Tanakh can be presented as a juxtaposition of these two archetypes. The same word 'anoint' is used for the king of Israel and for the prophet, while a slightly different word is used for the king of Aram (*umasahta* as opposed to *timsa*). In truth, the reality of political power is a mere shadow of the reality of spiritual power, which in turn is a shadow of the reality of being-itself, the becoming possible of the impossible. The word translated 'anoint' can also be translated 'smear', a mundane, everyday meaning, but used here in a spiritual context. Like many words, it has come to have an almost exclusively religious meaning, which has a misleading effect. Whether it is 'to smear' or 'to anoint' makes no difference from the point of view of being-itself. Neither is intrinsically holier or more God-like than the other.

Again, 'kill' symbolizes the rooting out of *kleshas*, the elimination of obstacles to awakening. Even Hazael has the power to do this, despite coming from a different religious background and not being a worshipper of YHWH, and probably not even a particularly nice person. Jehu represents an organized religion with some insight into non-duality, whereas Elisha will have a direct insight, like that of the Buddha knowing which teachings are relevant to each person. They all have a role to play—it may even be that Hazael and Jehu do most of the work, but it is Elisha who finishes the job.

'...[18] Yet I will leave seven thousand in Israel, all the knees that have not bowed to Baal, and every mouth that has not kissed him.'

Once again, we can only make tentative statements about numerology, but with that in mind we can be playful and speculative—the more interpretations the better. If we draw on Jewish and Buddhist traditions, seven thousand is one twelfth of eighty-four thousand, the total number of *kleshas* divided by the twelve tribes of Israel; so one 'tribe', a whole class of *kleshas*, has already been transformed from afflictive mind states—the dualism represented by Baal—with seventy-seven thousand to go. As there are eighty-four thousand *kleshas*, so there are eighty-four thousand teachings of the Buddha, each one representing an antidote to a specific *klesha*. Although this is speculative, seven thousand certainly represents something healthier than Elijah's claim he is the only one left. He has a sangha.

The reference to 'knees' and 'mouth' signifies those who pay homage to Baal as something external. In contrast, there is a relationship of equality between us and YHWH, because there is no dualistic separation. A friend of mine, who is an Anglican priest, has argued that worshippers should stand for the Eucharistic prayer to represent standing before God as equals, not sitting as though they were being entertained, but not kneeling as inferiors either. Although prostration is a common Buddhist practice, perhaps it isn't such a good practice, especially in front of a Buddha image. The King of Prayers says there is a Buddha on each atom, so why prostrate before some collections of atoms and not others? We are the Buddha's friends, his equals. The only difference is he got there before us, and in any case we are not separate from the Buddha-nature, the Dharmakaya, the Buddha. In some Buddhist countries, prostration is a common mark of respect, but where it is not part of the culture it can feel like a jarring import, and sometimes it looks and feels more showy than the humility or ego-control it is supposed to be.

Aversion to rituals and ceremonies is not a transcending of attachment to them. Our existence may be a shadow—there is no reality like YHWH's reality—but we share in the *same* reality, and it is to that ultimate reality (nirvana) we shall return. It is not a reward for anything, but it does mean realizing not-self, which is included in the Theravada understanding of *sotapanna* (stream-entry) alongside the transcending of attachment to rituals and ceremonies.

[19] *So he left that place, and found Elisha the son of Shaphat who was ploughing with twelve yoke of oxen before him, he with the twelfth. Elijah approached him and threw his mantle on him as he went past.*

Seemingly, Elijah doesn't bother to anoint the kings—this is left to Elisha and Elisha's servant.[6] He has realized enlightenment, but he hasn't reached the *final stage* of enlightenment according to the Zen ox-herding pictures, that of entering the marketplace with helping hands, like the 'true saint' of the Sufis, referred to earlier, who trades in the marketplace and participates in the life of the community, but never forgets God for a single moment.

It seems significant that Elisha is ploughing, as though he is meditating and expecting this to make him a Buddha, expecting to find God *by* seeking, expecting to polish a stone and make it into a mirror. The twelve yoke of oxen indicate he is throwing everything into this: his culture (twelve tribes) and his youth (twelve years). But none of that is what gets him there. He is a seeker, but it is not *by* seeking that he finds. Elijah throws the mantle over him in a rather off-hand way, in passing, leaving Elisha to catch up with him. Apparently, Elijah doesn't anoint him either, assuming anoint (or 'smear', as we saw earlier) means with oil. Or maybe we are meant to infer that the anointing is not an external ritual, but a *process* of real heart-to-heart transmission from teacher to disciple.

[20] *He left the oxen, ran after Elijah and said: 'Please let me kiss my father and mother, then I will follow you.' He said to him: 'Go back, for what have I done to you?'* [21] *He returned from following him, took the yoke of oxen and killed them, boiled their flesh with the yokes of the oxen, and gave to the people, who all ate. Then he arose and went after Elijah, and ministered to him.*

Elisha leaves the work of meditation, of polishing the stone. He asks Elijah to let him *kiss* his father and mother, a reminder that he has not kissed Baal. Elijah's response seems half-hearted, to put it mildly. The Buddha, after his awakening, was also reluctant to teach others. Elijah is asking Elisha to follow him *in the sense of succeeding him*, not to be in a teacher–pupil relationship but to be the next Buddha. Elisha, however, has other ideas. A teacher–pupil relationship needs to be instigated by the pupil, and there is a principle in Buddhism that *nobody* should teach until they have been asked to teach three times. Among Western Buddhists, there is sometimes a felt pressure to 'get a teacher', but the advice to watch a teacher carefully, for ten years even, is one that should be taken seriously. Elijah tries to put him off at first, which is also a good practice, comparable to the 'rejection' of prospective converts to Judaism—again, they have to ask three times.

Elijah's response can be compared with Jesus' much less compromising response to someone who wanted to do the same thing, to go back and say goodbye to his parents. Jesus commented that those who put their hand to the *plough* and look back are not worthy of the kingdom of heaven. Copying someone, even someone as great as Elisha, is not going to work. We can only be enlightened in person, as we can only go to the toilet in person. But Jesus also told the parable of the prodigal son, who left his father, and it was his return to the father that was presented as the archetype of salvation. Marco Pallis writes, in words that could summarize the entire story of Elijah:

The land of archetypes is the Pure Land. The Greek Fathers called it 'deification'...[U]niting with one's archetype is but to rejoin that which one already is 'in God,' to quote Meister Eckhart...The essential 'non-duality' of *samsâra* and nirvana is our proof that such is possible once that arch-prodigal, the samsaric wanderer, has made tracks for the parental home where the dreary cycle of birth and death may once and for all be ended.[7]

Elisha leaves everything, using his yoke as firewood — literally burning his livelihood — and feeding 'the people' with the meat of the oxen. He follows the Buddhist monastic practice of 'going forth into homelessness', and Jesus' later injunction to 'sell everything you have, give the money to the poor, and follow me'. There is an echo of the aftermath of King David's census, when David insisted on paying for the burnt offering himself, even though Araunah offered to give him oxen and yokes for firewood.[8]

Finally, we learn that Elisha 'ministered' to Elijah. This can also be translated 'became his servant', but it is not the same word used for his earlier servant, which reflects a different role. The emphasis is on *Elisha* as the one who provides service, who ministers, while Elijah's previous servant remains nameless. In Quaker meetings, the term 'ministry' is often used to refer to the act of speaking 'out of the silence' and sharing an 'insight' that has come to the speaker during the meeting. It is an act of service, and an act of prophecy. There is this ministry of speaking, and there is also a ministry of listening, but Elijah does not wait around for Elisha, because he has become a better teacher and does not rely on the pupil, or the servant, to validate his role (a temptation that faces spiritual teachers). There are different levels of symbolism here, and it is not that the servant symbolizes one thing rather than another.

Anger (1 Kings 20)

1 Kings 20 is a strange chapter, and probably the hardest part of the Elijah story to write about. There are many things in the story that problematize the notion of religion as founded on ethics. For example, being eaten by a lion for not striking someone is not justice, whatever some commentators might think, and hopefully none of them will ever be on a jury. Again, however, it makes more sense when the characters are understood as representing mind states or archetypes. By not uprooting the *klesha* known as Ben-hadad, Ahab himself (or what he represents—materialism, dualism) is uprooted. Ben-hadad means son of the blacksmith, or son of the thunder God (one of the same pantheon as Baal), or son of thunder (like James and John in the Gospels), or son of noise. He represents anger; he is the Donald Trump of the Elijah story. It is also strange because Elijah is not named in this chapter, though one or both of the unnamed prophets (the ones who are not killed by a lion, that is) could be him, especially if (as is possible) this chapter is out of chronological order within the Elijah story. But the absence of Elijah could also highlight a kind of emptiness, as we sometimes become aware of a background noise (like the noise of an electric fan) only when it suddenly stops. There is also no reference to Baal or Baal worship in this chapter.

> **20** *Ben-hadad the king of Aram gathered all his army together. He had thirty-two kings with him, and horses and chariots. He went up and besieged Samaria, and fought against it.*

'Ben-hadad the king of Aram'—Elijah has been told to anoint Hazael as king of Aram, so immediately we know that Ben-hadad's days are numbered and that he is, in a sense, an illegitimate ruler. The *klesha* of anger is not our true nature; if it were, we could show it at any time.[1] So it is an illegitimate ruler, and its days are numbered for someone who has become a stream-enterer, which *Elijah* has—so Elijah is present in this chapter when it is read psychologically, in the Buddhist-inspired way that shapes this commentary.

He 'gathered all his army together. He had thirty-two kings with him, and horses and chariots'—demonstrating the apparent power of this *klesha*, that it can bring thirty-two subsidiary *kleshas* with it. In Buddhist philosophy, anger is one of the 'root afflictions', a *klesha* that is a major cause of other *kleshas*. In this passage, it is not clear which *kleshas*, but they are tributaries to their suzerain, anger. We can speculate that the thirty-two physical characteristics of the Buddha represent the opposition, the antidotes, to those *kleshas*. Ben-hadad's armies 'went up and besieged Samaria, and fought against it'—so it is not only an *apparent* power but an *active* power, capable of doing real damage. However, it is ultimately unreal, and its days are numbered. As the Hindu prayer says, *asato ma sat gemaya*, lead me from the unreal to the real.

> [2] *He sent messengers into the city, to Ahab king of Israel,* [3] *who said to him: 'Ben-hadad says this: Your silver and gold is mine, also your wives and your children, even the best of them, are mine.'* [4] *The king of Israel answered and said: 'It is as you say, my lord, O king: I am yours, and all that I have.'* [5] *The messengers came again, and said: 'Ben-hadad says this, saying: I have indeed sent word to you, saying: You will deliver me your silver and gold, and your wives and children...'*

The phrase 'Ben-hadad says this' is juxtaposed with the phrase 'YHWH says this', used several times in the Elijah narrative; its repeated use indicates and emphasizes Ben-hadad's inflated sense of his own importance, highlighting his role as the Donald Trump of the Elijah story. Non-duality involves humility; it is not a cataphatic pantheism that insists 'I am God'. Nevertheless, he sends 'messengers'—*malakim*, the same word translated as 'messenger' and 'angel' in chapter 19. Anger cannot communicate by itself, either in an I–Thou or an I–It relationship.[2] According to the Buddhist text the *Abhidharmasamuccaya*: 'It has the function of causing oneself not to remain in contact with happiness.'[3] This is why it is such an afflicted state of mind and destined to be uprooted, or, rather, transformed and redeemed.

We should think more about this. Are the *kleshas* to be rooted out and destroyed, or transformed and redeemed? Is it even an either/or? Thich Nhat Hanh implies it is not, when he says 'God transcends all notions, including the notions of creation and destruction.'[4] The text here is agonistic, but it subtly points us to transformation and redemption. It is the '*klesha*-ness' of anger that is to be destroyed, but anger itself is to be transformed and redeemed (as in Tantric Buddhism).

Ben-hadad—anger—is not only acquisitive, but also has a sense of entitlement. Before the Elijah story, the king of Judah sent Ben-hadad silver and gold to persuade him not to ally with Israel against Judah.[5] It has become an addiction for Ben-hadad, because of his sense of entitlement and self-importance, which in turn is because of his anger. He even emphasizes the point by taking this sense of entitlement further: 'also your wives and your children, even the best of them, are mine.' Ahab's sense of self-preservation leads him to agree immediately. He doesn't yet realize that feeding this *klesha* will only make it hungrier. As an addict, Ben-hadad develops a tolerance to the object of his addiction, thereby needing more and more.

'...[6] *but I will send my servants to you at this time tomorrow, and they will search your house and the houses of your servants. Whatever is pleasant to you, they will put in their hand and take away.*'

85

It has escalated further. Ahab's attempt at appeasement has failed. The *klesha* has been promised a feed, and that has only made it hungrier. We should note that the phrase 'Whatever is pleasant to you' could alternatively be read 'Whatever is pleasant to *them*' — the former is in the Hebrew text, the latter in the Septuagint, Syriac and Vulgate texts. The former translation is the more dramatic, however, because it implies a strong degree of schadenfreude, taking something merely because it is pleasing to its owner, inflicting loss for the sake of causing unhappiness. This is further evidence of where anger can lead.

Many Western responses to Buddhism attempt to minimize its teachings on anger, seeing it as a psychologically-healthy catharsis. There is a need for balance here. There is a genuine danger in denying our anger, or burying it, but it really is a *klesha*, indeed a *root* affliction. As well as balance, we need to be specific: the *klesha* here is allied with *power* (like that of Trump), and the Buddhist teachings should not lead us to conceptualize anger-with-power in the same way as anger-without-power. When Jesus said that anger with a brother or sister would lead to judgement[6] (that is, negative karma), he was referring to a top-down anger being inflicted on an equal. But he demonstrated an anger on behalf of the poor and powerless when he overturned the tables of the moneychangers in the Temple.[7] In Tantric Buddhism, anger (like desire and ignorance) can be *used*, as an aid in the path to liberation.[8]

> [7] *Then the king of Israel called all the elders of the land and said to them: See how this man seeks trouble? He demanded my wives and children, silver and gold, and I did not deny him.'* [8] *All the elders and all the people said to him: 'Do not listen, and do not consent.'* [9] *Therefore, he said to the messengers of Ben-hadad: 'Tell my lord the king: I your servant will meet all your earlier demands, but this I cannot do.' The messengers departed, and brought word back to him.*

The reason the *klesha*'s days are numbered is that eventually its victims are going to resist, and anger will not have a coherent plan to defeat them. It rules by fear alone. Eventually, even those who have most to lose will realize they have nothing to lose. By threatening to take everything, Ben-hadad removes the incentive to surrender and submit. Ahab is still willing to negotiate, but Ben-hadad is threatening his sense of self-preservation. Ahab makes one last effort to maintain his delusion. The word for 'messenger' is still the same as the word for 'angel'. However, Ahab emphasizes not an unwillingness but an *inability* to comply ('this I *cannot* do'). Brueggemann suggests that even his royal authority does not give him the power to overrule the elders and people on this issue.[9] Ahab's problem is that he is treating the *klesha* as *rational*—in the sociological sense of able to calculate means and ends—like his own sense of self-preservation.

[10] *Ben-hadad sent word to him and said: 'So let the Gods do to me, and more also, if there is enough dust left in Samaria for a handful for each of the people who follow me.'*

Ben-hadad reflects Jezebel's earlier words: 'So let the Gods do to me, and more also, if I do not make your life like their lives by this time tomorrow.' They are different *kleshas* but they behave in similar ways, with an overinflated sense of their own importance, believing themselves to be necessary, to be life itself. Again—typically of this *klesha*—Ben-hadad indulges in hyperbole, not only threatening to reduce Samaria to dust, but to destroy even the dust itself.

[11] *The king of Israel answered: 'Tell him: The one who puts on armor should not boast like the one who takes it off.'* [12] *When Ben-hadad heard this message, as he was drinking, he and the kings, in the booths, he said to his servants: 'Get yourselves in position.' And they got themselves in position against the city.*

Is Ahab taunting Ben-hadad, accusing him of being a coward? This seems unwise, not to mention out of character for Ahab, but it could set Ben-hadad's anger and ambition against each other, in that his anger is lacking in calculated self-interest or self-preservation, while his desire to win is dependent on those things. He is drunk on anger and ambition, not using skillful means. The thirty-two kings/*kleshas* are also drunk.

> [13] *A prophet came near to Ahab king of Israel and said: 'YHWH says this: Have you seen this great multitude? I will deliver it into your hand today, and you will know that I am YHWH.'* [14] *Ahab said: 'By whom?' And he said: 'YHWH says this: By the young men of the princes of the provinces.' Then he said: 'Who will begin the battle?' And he answered: 'You.'*

'A prophet'—is this Elijah or someone else? If it is Elijah he has gone from being 'Elijah the Tishbite' to 'Elijah the prophet' to a nameless prophet. This could represent his labyrinthine journey to enlightenment, an apparent demotion masking an actual progression. Or maybe Mount Horeb has led to some insight into, and realization of, *anatta*—symbolized by a namelessness that reflects the ultimate namelessness of God. If it is someone else, it is *evidence* that Elijah is not the only one left—the reference to seven thousand in the last chapter may emphasize this, though there is no indication that was about prophets, enlightened ones, arahants, *sotapannas*. More likely they were 'hearers' (*upasika/upasaka*), people ready to hear the teachings of the enlightened prophets. The phrase 'YHWH says this' is a rejoinder to Ben-hadad, being-itself replying to anger. The name YHWH is emphasized by being used three times in these two verses.

'Have you seen this great multitude? I will deliver it into your hand today, and you will know that I am YHWH'—because YHWH is 'I am', being-itself, the ground of being, so there is a sense in which the enlightened mind is given everything. But will Ahab be ready? Would even Elijah be ready at this point?

What follows may look like a detail of military strategy, but the starring role is given to 'the young men of the princes of the provinces', that is, the servants of Ahab's servants. There is a Sufi story of Abraham seeing Gabriel write a list of the friends of God, and asking if his name was on the list. When Gabriel said 'no', Abraham said, 'I am a friend of the friends of God.' After a long silence, Gabriel announced he had been instructed to write Abraham's name at the top of the list. Was this because of Abraham's humility, or because he regarded himself as one with God, since God is the one friend of the friends of God? The answer must be both. It is not the head (the hard-headed Ahab), but the feet that bring the whole body into enlightenment. This is emphasized in the Gospels and other parts of the New Testament: 'God has chosen the foolish things in the world to shame the wise, and the weak to shame the strong. God has chosen the low-born and despised things of the world, and the things that are not to bring to nothing the things that are'.[10] Nevertheless, Ahab is told to take the initiative, and he is *ready*. There is a dialectic of action and grace.

> [15] *Then he counted the young men of the princes of the provinces, and they were two hundred and thirty-two, and after them he counted all the people, all the children of Israel being seven thousand.*

The numbers are symbolic: two hundred and thirty-two young men compared with the thirty-two kings; and 'all the children of Israel' numbering seven thousand, the same number who had not knelt before Baal and kissed him, or one twelfth (one tribe) of the eighty-four thousand antidotes to the eighty-four thousand *kleshas*. It is not all the people of Ahab's kingdom, but those who struggle with God.

¹⁶ They went out at noon. But Ben-hadad was drinking himself drunk in the booths, he and the kings, the thirty-two kings who were supporting him.

'They went out at noon', the time of the noon prayer, highlighting daytime consciousness, when prayer and action are not two. It is broad daylight; they are not taking on anger surreptitiously, but openly and directly. Again Ben-hadad is drunk, as anger is a form of drunkenness, drunk on self-importance and entitlement. Perhaps this is a meaning of the fifth lay precept in Buddhism. The precept is usually translated in terms of avoiding alcohol and intoxicants, but the Pali refers to *sura, meraya* and *majja*, and it is not entirely clear what substances they refer to, leading to an attitude of avoiding all intoxicants—including alcohol—in order to play it safe. However, the next word in the precept—*pamadatthana*—can mean 'which lead to heedlessness' or 'insofar as they lead to heedlessness', and this would seem to mean heedlessness of others, which is consistent with the other four precepts (killing, stealing, sexual misconduct, lying[11]), and also consistent with the Buddhist teachings on anger.

¹⁷ The young men of the princes of the provinces went out first, and Ben-hadad also sent people out. They told him: 'There are men who have come out from Samaria.' ¹⁸ He said: 'If they have come out for peace, take them alive, or if they have come out for war, take them alive.' ¹⁹ So the young men of the princes of the provinces went out of the city, and the army that followed them...

Ben-hadad is somewhat incoherent, because his drunken anger makes him incapable of seeing anything as it is. He can only project his own desires and sense of entitlement, so he needs to send people out. We might expect his anger to dictate that he order those coming out of Samaria to be killed, but his arrogance seemingly takes precedence over his anger here. All of this leads to a slowness; it will soon be too late for him.

>...²⁰ killed one enemy soldier each. The Arameans fled and Israel pursued them. Ben-hadad the king of Aram escaped on a horse with horsemen. ²¹ The king of Israel went out, attacked the horses and chariots, and killed the Arameans with a great slaughter. ²² The prophet came near to the king of Israel and said to him: 'Go, strengthen yourself, take note and see what you have done, for at the turn of the year the king of Aram will come up against you.'

Ben-hadad finally sees things as they are. There are losses for him, but he escapes. Anger has been defeated in battle but not overcome. The other *kleshas* are overcome, but they are the secondary afflictions, the *kleshas* that are subject to anger (to Ben-hadad); they are not anger itself. Defeating or transforming anger is a long-term endeavor. One battle is not enough. And it is anger that will attack, so there is a need to be ready for it, and to take note of *how* it has attacked in the past.

>²³ The servants of the king of Aram said to him: 'Their God is a God of the hills, which is why they were stronger than us, but let us fight them on the plain, and then we shall surely be stronger than them. ²⁴ Take the kings away and put governors in their place. ²⁵ Count out an army, like the army that you have lost: horse for horse and chariot for chariot. We will fight against them on the plain, and we shall surely be stronger than them.' He listened, and did what they said.

The reference to 'their Gods' shows a misunderstanding of YHWH's unity, and a henotheistic idea of *cuius regio euis religio*. Anger seeks excuses for its own failures. The vassal kings/ *kleshas* are not trusted any more, even though they support anger. They are replaced by clones of Ben-hadad, *kleshas* made in the image of anger, which really means thirty-three *kleshas* have been reduced to one. Because Ben-hadad and his advisers have shifted the blame, they think it is possible to do the same thing ('horse for horse, and chariot for chariot') and expect a different result. Again, this is evidence of the irrationality of anger, despite its power and strength.

26 At the turn of the year, Ben-hadad mustered the Arameans and went up to Aphek, to fight against Israel.

As predicted earlier, this happens 'at the turn of the year', which should be a time for new intentions, but anger refuses to start afresh, preferring to revert to old habits and resentments. Some translations say it was in spring, but it could be in autumn, the time of Rosh Hashanah.[12] It would have been preceded by reflecting on one's sins of the previous year, meaning one's mistakes, or, more literally, times when one has missed the mark—like missing the bull's eye but hitting the target, or failing to kill the animal cleanly but wounding it, leading to pain and suffering and a drawn-out death. But Ben-hadad doesn't feel the need for this, like Trump when he claimed he didn't need to ask God's forgiveness for anything.

27 The children of Israel were mustered and given rations, and went against them. The children of Israel camped before them like two little flocks of goats, but the Arameans filled the land.

The Israelites seem happy to meet in the place chosen by Ben-hadad, even though 'the Arameans filled the land', the *eretz*. Neither terrain nor circumstances nor vicissitudes are decisive in the battle between the *kleshas* and the journey to enlightenment. In Buddhism, the eight vicissitudes are pleasure and pain, gain and loss, praise and blame, and fame and disrepute—and the *Brahma vihara* (divine abode) of equanimity is the ability to remain unperturbed by these circumstances, which are always temporary. The 'children of Israel' were 'like two little flocks of kids'—a possible wordplay emphasizing their apparent weakness, like David against Goliath, so this *klesha* is to be defeated through weakness, not through strength. But why *two* flocks of kids? This refers to the Israelites, not to the Israelites and the Arameans. Does it refer to the worshippers of YHWH alone and the (Israelite) worshippers of Baal and Asherah? Does it denote a dualism that will nonetheless lead them into non-duality? Does it refer to method and wisdom? Skillful means and unbending principles? All of these are possible, and they all need to be combined into one flock.[13]

> [28] *A man of God came near and said to the king of Israel: 'YHWH says this: Because the Arameans have said that YHWH is a God of the hills but not a God of the valleys, therefore I will deliver all this great multitude into your hand, and you will know that I am YHWH.'*

This verse doesn't refer to a prophet but to 'a man of God', a man of the *Elohim*, so he is indistinguishable from a man of the Gods, reflecting the interchangeability of 'God' and 'the Gods' in the ancient world and in modern Hinduism that is mentioned earlier, as well as the *logical* principle that if x is God and y is God then x and y are the same God, so all Gods are one. This doesn't look accidental, so is YHWH speaking through someone who would not otherwise be seen as a prophet, someone from outside the Abrahamic tradition? Enlightenment can come from all sorts of places, some 'sacred', some 'profane', some 'sudden', some 'gradual'. It can only come from where we are.

He is a man of the *Elohim*, but he speaks in the name of YHWH. His statement is not henotheistic but is in explicit contrast to the principle of *cuius regio eius religio*. If the God of the hills is God and the God of the valleys is God then the God of the hills and the God of the valleys are the same God. If the *Elohim* is/are God and YHWH is God then the *Elohim* and YHWH are the same God. The man repeats the formula 'and you will know that I am YHWH', pointing to enlightenment, direct perception of being-itself, which is neither personal nor less than personal. He attributes the words 'because YHWH' to the Arameans, whereas they actually said 'because the *Elohe'* (God or Gods). There seems to be some misrepresentation here, a theme we consider later.

²⁹ *They camped over and against them for seven days. On the seventh day the battle was joined, and the children of Israel killed one hundred thousand Aramean foot soldiers in one day. ³⁰ But the rest fled to Aphek, into the city, and the wall fell on twenty-seven thousand who were left. Ben-hadad fled, and came into the city, into an inner chamber.*

Encampment for seven days is reminiscent of the battle of Jericho.[14] They are camped 'over and against' each other, opposite and oppositional. There is dualism here, even if it is a dualism of non-duality and duality, but once again this is a stage on the journey to complete non-duality, a fullness of non-duality which subsumes the other non-dualities within it.

The number one hundred thousand must be symbolic, and certainly hyperbolic. But they are 'foot soldiers', minor *kleshas*, such that killing even one hundred thousand of them is not equal to rooting out (or transforming and redeeming) the one *klesha* of anger itself. The others try to take shelter, but it is this very act of self-preservation, self-grasping, that destroys them. Again, this is reminiscent of Jericho, whose inhabitants took shelter within the city, leading to their destruction.[15] But still Ben-hadad has not been destroyed.

³¹ His servants said to him: 'We have heard that the kings of Israel are merciful. Please, let us put sackcloth round our waists and ropes on our heads, and go to the king of Israel. Perhaps he will save your life.' ³² So they wrapped sackcloth round their waists and put ropes on their heads, and came to the king of Israel and said: 'Your servant Ben-hadad says: Please let me live.' He said: 'Is he still alive? He is my brother.'

Ben-hadad's servants portray the mercy of the Israelite kings (note the plural) as both a virtue and a weakness. They minimize the threat or danger that anger poses. Indeed, mercy is a virtue, but here it is mercy toward a *klesha* at just the time it can be rooted out. Ahab's comment 'He is my brother' reflects the view of anger common in the West, that it is a healthy thing, which is in turn dependent on a certainty of our own rightness— 'we' have reason to be angry. This reflects the psychological concept of the fundamental attribution error, our own behavior (particularly negative behavior) being explained in terms of circumstances, and other people's in terms of disposition. But it also reflects what Solzhenitsyn said about the line between good and evil:

If only it were all so simple! If only there were evil people somewhere insidiously committing evil deeds, and it were necessary only to separate them from the rest of us and destroy them. But the line dividing good and evil cuts through the heart of every human being. And who is willing to destroy a piece of his own heart?[16]

This is complicated. In the story of Elijah there is a sometimes uncomfortable non-duality of virtue and non-virtue, of good and evil, which problematizes the notion of religion as founded on ethics. In Coleman Barks's rendering of Rumi, he writes about meeting each other in a field beyond ideas of right and wrong.[17] Note that he doesn't write about meeting in a field beyond right and wrong, but beyond *ideas* of right and wrong, *ideas* of good and evil, not beyond good and evil *per se*. And we cannot go beyond ideas of good and evil without first going *through* those ideas. Avoiding the subject altogether, treating it as taboo, is really a kind of laziness. It is something we need to think about, even if we might (and probably should) come to different conclusions.

Mark Rowlands, in his memoir *The Philosopher and the Wolf*, cites the shuttlebox as an exemplar of human evil, a device for creating 'learned helplessness' in dogs by the repeated application of electric shocks. In the same book, he cites Colin McGinn's understanding of evil as schadenfreude. For me, evil is encapsulated in a casual cruelty, casual in that it is held to be of no real consequence, as in the film *Welcome to Sarajevo*, when one character speaks almost nonchalantly of killing someone, saying, 'It was not too bad. I don't know...therapeutic.' In all three cases, evil seems to be revealed in our treatment of the weak.

The great Quaker minister Elias Hicks said that evil begins with 'an excess in the indulgence of propensities', even though those propensities 'in themselves...are all good; because man could not give himself propensities or desires.'[18] Perhaps he was inspired by the Jewish tradition that sees evil as an excess of justice; the best illustration of this that I can think of is Camus's excoriation of the death penalty:

Many laws consider a premeditated crime more serious than a crime of pure violence. But what then is capital punishment but the most premeditated of murders, to which no criminal's deed, however calculated it may be, can be compared? For there to be equivalence, the death penalty would have to punish a criminal who had warned his victim of the date at which he would inflict a horrible death on him and who, from that moment onward, had confined him at his mercy for months. Such a monster is not encountered in private life.[19]

Although (as we shall see) this chapter in the story of Elijah suggests that Ahab does the wrong thing with respect to Ben-hadad, it is not hard to sympathize with him. Indeed, it would be psychopathic not to. But we need to remember what Ahab represents—self-preservation rather than a universal ethical principle—and it is *this* that motivates him here, *not* the virtue of mercy. He possibly thinks that uprooting one major *klesha* would set a precedent for the *klesha* that *he* represents.

> [33] *Now Ahab's men took this as a sign, and quickly grasped it from him, so they said: 'Your brother Ben-hadad.' Then he said: 'Go and bring him here.' Then Ben-hadad came to him, and he caused him to come up into his chariot.* [34] *Ben-hadad said to him: 'I will restore the cities my father took from your father, and you may set up marketplaces in Damascus, as my father set up marketplaces in Samaria.' Ahab said 'I will let you go with this covenant.' So he made a covenant with him, and let him go.*

The complex nature of this means it is no clearer to Ahab's men, so they watch for a sign. Rather than being signposts,[20] they tell Ahab what they think he wants to hear. The self-appointed hard-headed realist can easily get into that sort of relationship with others, so hard-headed realism is not so easily distinguishable from cowardice (moral and actual) or fear (which is nonetheless well-disguised).

He comes up into the chariot. It is not clear which king comes up into which king's chariot, which is probably a deliberate ambiguity. Ahab's chariot was mentioned earlier, but there is also a contrast with the chariot at the end of the story of

Elijah. There is a time for us to make friends with our *kleshas*, but this is allowing them to make friends with each other. This is emphasized by the covenant or treaty between them, which, furthermore, is a materialistic one. There is no mention of YHWH, no indication Ahab has learned 'that I am YHWH'. Indeed, the reference to 'covenant' suggests Ahab has forgotten the covenant with YHWH.

[35] *A certain man of the sons of the prophets said to another one by the word of YHWH: 'Please strike me.' The man refused to strike him.*

In at least two of her books, Karen Armstrong discusses the effect that being called as a prophet sometimes had on people. The divine could be experienced as a disruptive force, an uprooting, a shattering blow:[21]

...for the Axial Age prophets, God was often experienced as a devastating shock. Isaiah was filled with mortal terror when he had a vision of God in the Temple; Jeremiah knew the divine as a pain that convulsed his limbs, broke his heart and made him stagger around like a drunk. The whole career of Ezekiel, who may have been a contemporary of Gotama, illustrates the radical discontinuity that now existed between the Sacred on the one hand, and the conscious, self-protecting self, on the other: God afflicted the prophet with such anxiety that he could not stop trembling; when his wife died, God forbade him to mourn; God forced him to eat excrement and to walk around town with packed bags like a refugee. Sometimes, in order to enter the divine presence, it seemed necessary to deny the normal responses of a civilized individual and to do violence to the mundane self.[22]

This undermines any idea that the journey to enlightenment is nice and easy, comfortable and predictable—yet the difficulty is for the ego, not the clear and knowing mind, for which it is like a fish's journey downstream to the sea. The man who refuses to strike the prophet has an *ethical* reaction—in Kierkegaard's terms ethical but not *religious*, as Abraham's reaction would have been had he refused to sacrifice his son in obedience to God's command. Kierkegaard's distinction can be compared to the distinction between relative and absolute *bodhicitta*, the former being rooted in everyday compassion, the latter in a perceptual realization of emptiness.

The phrase 'sons of the prophets' appears again toward the end of the story, and we will consider its meaning then. It also reflects the earlier reference to 'the sons of Jacob'.

> [36] *Then he said to him: 'Because you have not listened to the voice of YHWH, as soon as you leave me a lion will kill you.' And as soon as he left him, a lion found him and killed him.* [37] *Then he found another man and said: 'Please strike me.' The man struck him, striking and wounding him.*

Again, the killing of the 'ethically-correct' man is not an act of justice, but an excess of justice. We are not to take it literally, but sometimes we do need to put ethics—in a codified sense—in second place in order to be faithful to God, acting as a bodhisattva maintaining the path through difficult terrain, so others can use it. In the small town where I grew up, there was a man who walked the same route every day, solely to ensure it remained a legal right of way; sometimes we walk for no other reason than to bless the desert spaces in between. James Fowler mentions a 'devotion to universalizing compassion' that 'may offend our parochial perceptions of justice'.[23] God is not the 'steward of morality', to use Reb Zalman's words, however many religious assumptions this might violate, and however inexplicable its consequences might be.

Why a lion? I think lion here symbolizes courage.[24] The man's ethical correctness is swallowed up by courage, which is here represented as a *religious* value (in Kierkegaard's sense). Elijah may be missing from the explicit narrative, but we are seeing the same process of transformation that we see throughout the story. Many of the *kleshas* that are rooted out are almost self-evidently non-virtuous, but even virtue can be an obstacle to enlightenment. In meditation, people often get distracted by virtuous (or what they and their community consider to be virtuous) thoughts, and this takes them away from the work at hand, which may be focusing on the breath, or reciting the mantra, allowing the prayer gradually to pray itself. These thoughts are not bad in themselves, which is why they are called virtuous, but in this context they really are obstacles. The other man does the ethically-wrong but (again in Kierkegaard's sense) religiously-right thing.

[38] *So the prophet left and waited for the king by the way. He disguised himself with his headband over his eyes.*

He is no longer 'a certain man of the sons of the prophets', but a prophet. His enlightenment has been sudden, like a blow from someone else's fist. Things are still a bit unclear, but it is clear he has something in mind. Why would a headband over his *eyes* act as a disguise, rather than a hindrance to the prophet himself? Either he is a prophet known to Ahab (in which case he could well be Elijah), or there is something in the eyes of the prophets that marks him out as one. The eye of a prophet, or seer, would represent a clear and knowing wisdom against which any *klesha* would be helpless, so it is disguised as a wound, an affliction, a weakness, so that the Ahab *klesha* will be enticed to pay attention.

³⁹ As the king passed by, he cried to the king and said: 'Your servant went out into the middle of the battle, when a man handed another man to me and said: Keep this man. If for any reason he goes missing then it will be your life for his life, or else you will pay a talent of silver...'

He is not telling the truth, but this emphasizes the importance of storytelling in conveying the dharma. This is sometimes forgotten in Western Buddhism, though it is much more important in Asian Buddhism (e.g. the Jataka tales, Zen stories, the life story of the Buddha). The equating of a life with a talent of silver highlights the materialism of Ahab's deal with Benhadad.

'...⁴⁰ And as your servant was busily occupied, he escaped.' The king of Israel said to him: 'Then that is how your judgement will be; you yourself have decided it.'

It may seem as though Ahab is applying a legitimate principle here, but really he is simply rushing to judgement. Indeed, he says 'you yourself have decided it', though it is not clear from the prophet's story—even had it been factual—that he agreed to the other man's terms.

⁴¹ He hurriedly took the headband away from his eyes, and the king of Israel discerned that he was one of the prophets.

As hinted earlier, the eyes immediately lead Ahab to recognize him, the *klesha* to recognize the enlightened mind, like the demons recognized Jesus.[25]

⁴² He said to Ahab: 'YHWH says this: Because you let the man I devoted to destruction go from out of your hand, it will be your life for his life, and your people for his people.'

Another use of the phrase 'YHWH says this', and it is Ahab's own measure of justice that comes back to him. Jesus makes a similar point in the Sermon on the Mount, that the measure we apply to others will be applied to us, if we forgive we will be forgiven.[26] This is deeply karmic: what Ahab considers to be karma for someone else is also karma for him, and his apparent mercy to Ben-hadad is revealed not to be mercy, since he is so unmerciful to a man who seems weak, a social inferior, of no threat to him—and this is in contrast to God's preferential option for the poor that is shown in the next chapter. It also becomes clear that Ahab's failure to destroy the anger *klesha* will have consequences for him, the representative of self-preservation and self-grasping.

> [43] *The king of Israel went back to his house in Samaria, sullen and dispirited.*

Ahab's reaction is understandable, since by conventional standards he has behaved ethically and the prophet has behaved dishonestly, but he doesn't realize it is his own measure of justice that has come back to him, nor that his codified ethic is quite different from enlightenment. He doesn't move forward on the path, so he goes *back*, back to Samaria, to what is familiar and safe, typical of the Ahab *klesha*. The phrase 'sullen and dispirited' reappears in the next chapter—they are both subsidiaries of the Ahab *klesha*. In a way, this contrasts with anger, because it is implosive rather than explosive. It seems that the *kleshas* are being mapped out in some detail here, as they are in the *Abhidharmasamuccaya* and other Buddhist texts.

The Politics of *Anatta* (1 Kings 21)

21 After these things, it so happened that Naboth the Jezreelite had a vineyard, which was in Jezreel, right by the palace of Ahab, king of Samaria.

The author of the text makes a point of saying that the events of this chapter occurred 'after these things', which presumably means later than the events in chapter 20, and probably later than chapters 17–19, though it is not certain that the story of Elijah is meant to be understood chronologically. Assuming it is later than chapters 17–19, the references to 'Elijah the Tishbite' in this chapter take on a particular meaning, as we shall see.

The name Naboth means 'words' or 'prophecies' (related to *nevi'im*) and Jezreel means 'El sows', so Naboth the Jezreelite means prophecies that El sows. Not YHWH, because they are experienced, phenomenologically, as sown by El, the presiding deity, the supreme being rather than being-itself, but they are really, ontologically, sown by YHWH. Naboth had a vineyard (which has to be 'sown'), symbolic of those prophecies and of a rich communion with YHWH. There is a significance in its being a vineyard, a place for producing wine. Wine is a common theme in the Tanakh and the New Testament, and its apparent prohibition in Buddhism needs to be understood symbolically, both in terms of anger (as we saw earlier), and as not settling for the lesser drunkenness. In Sufi discourse, the greater drunkenness, or intoxication, is the love of God to the point of oneness with God, in which the 'unhinged lover' (to use Caputo's words, cited in the introduction to this book) has eyes only for the beloved. In certain tantric contexts, the consumption of small amounts of alcohol is not only permitted but obligatory. This is also true in Judaism (especially at Purim), and in the Christian Eucharist (though some denominations use alcohol-free wine or even fruit juice). A former student of mine said he wasn't religious, but if he were to become religious he would choose Islam because, he said, 'Islam is strong wine.'

The vineyard is right beside the palace, but not part of it, because these prophecies are truth spoken to power, to comfort the afflicted and afflict the comfortable. This is a hint of what is to come, that this will be the most political episode in the story of Elijah and more 'typically' prophetic, with analogies to other prophets of the Tanakh, especially Amos.

> [2] *And Ahab said to Naboth: 'Give me your vineyard, so that I may have it as a herb garden, because it is near to my house. I will give you a better vineyard in exchange or, if you prefer, I will give you its value in money.'* [3] *Naboth said to Ahab: 'YHWH forbid that I should give you my fathers' inheritance.'*

Ben-hadad's sense of entitlement seems to have rubbed off on Ahab, who thinks he can buy the word of God, the dharma, being-itself made human language. Such a vineyard is priceless, worth everything we have and everything we are. Yet Ahab's materialistic mind leads him to suggest that such a thing can be bought. Naboth says he can't sell it, for it would run against the terms of his inheritance (he holds the vineyard in trust) — the prophecies or words of YHWH are not his property to give away, and he recognizes this.

> [4] *Ahab went back to his house sullen and dispirited because Naboth the Jezreelite had said to him: 'I will not give you my fathers' inheritance.' He lay down on his bed, turned his face away, and refused to eat.* [5] *But Jezebel his wife came to him and said: 'Why is your spirit so depressed that you are refusing to eat?'*

The words 'sullen and dispirited' are repeated from the end of the previous chapter. Ahab doesn't become angry like Ben-hadad, but sinks into a state of self-absorption, torpor and possibly clinical depression. His refusal to eat is a sign Ahab is not always motivated by self-preservation. Is this progress or not? It is hard to say. According to Jezebel, he is indeed 'depressed'. This is the same word that was translated 'dispirited' earlier, but a different declension. Jezebel represents Mara, greed, a sure sign things are about to escalate.

> *6 He said to her: 'Because I said to Naboth the Jezreelite: Give me your vineyard for money or, if you prefer, I will give you another vineyard in exchange; and he answered: I will not give you my vineyard.' 7 Jezebel his wife said to him: 'Do you now govern the kingdom of Israel? Rise up and eat, and let your heart be happy. I will give you the vineyard of Naboth the Jezreelite.' 8 So she wrote letters in Ahab's name, sealed them with his seal, and sent them to the elders and nobles in his city, who lived with Naboth.*

Jezebel uses his sense of self-importance ('Do you now govern the kingdom of Israel?') and proceeds in accordance with greed. Again, this is not 'normal' materialism as in a sense of self-preservation, but something more. According to Brueggemann, this is a social ideology that accompanies theological Baalism, 'wherein Jezebel holds to and practices a theory of land ownership that privileges royal claims'.[1] So it is not surprising that Jezebel really does seem to believe the vineyard is hers to take and hers to give. The politics of *anatta*—the political implications of not-self, which include God's preferential option for the poor—can have nothing to do with Jezebel's politics, but Jezebel's attitude even contrasts with *Ahab's* initial recognition (albeit reluctant and resentful) that the vineyard is not there for the taking. She goes as far as to take over Ahab's rightful power—the hard-headed materialism is being overtaken by a Randian greed-is-good ethos. This is also a clear indication of dishonesty, which is about to get worse.

[9] *In those letters, she wrote: 'Proclaim a fast, set Naboth at the head of the people...'*

At this point in Jezebel's story, her motives contrast with those of Ahab. His earlier fast is associated with depression, and elsewhere fasting is associated with *taqwa*, God-consciousness, but here it is something insidious and manipulative. It may be connected with Baal worship, attempting to whip up a heightened sense of duality and create a sense of threat, in order to emphasize the urgency of dealing with this threat—what Naomi Klein calls a 'shock doctrine'.[2]

Naboth is seated at the head of the assembly. This could symbolize the prophecies being given a place of honor, but with the intention of discrediting them dishonestly. Alternatively, it could mean the place where the accused is on trial, like the dock in an English courtroom. Ancient and modern commentators disagree on this point, and some suggest the text is deliberately ambiguous. But assuming the former interpretation, it is comparable to deliberate attempts to misrepresent the dharma (Buddhist or Abrahamic) in order to make it appear stupid and life-denying, in order to justify something more materialistic.

'...[10] and set two men, worthless ones, before him, and let them bear witness against him, saying: You cursed God and the king. And then carry him out and stone him, so he will die.'

The dishonesty becomes clear. The 'worthless' men are literally 'sons of Belial', which in post-exilic times would be identified with the Devil, Mara. Naboth is alleged to have 'cursed God'— *Elohim*, i.e. 'the Gods', not explicitly distinguished from YHWH, but nonetheless more in keeping with Jezebel's dualistic version of polytheism. This is evidence of where self-entitlement and greed can lead if they are combined together—Ahab's old self-preservation would probably not have gone this far on its own.

¹¹ The men of his city, that is, the elders and nobles who lived there, did as Jezebel had said, according to what was written in the letters she had sent. ¹² They proclaimed a fast, and set Naboth at the head of the people. ¹³ The two men, the worthless ones, came in and sat before him, and the worthless men bore witness against Naboth in the presence of the people, saying: 'Naboth cursed God and the king.' Then they carried him out of the city, and stoned him with stones, so that he died.

Ahab's earlier words to Jezebel are a repetition of his earlier actions, whereas here the actions are a repetition of the earlier words. This is similar to some early Buddhist texts which seem to use refrains like this in order to make memorization easier. Was the story of Elijah meant to be sung, in the style of Tibetan songs of experience, for example?

¹⁴ Then they sent word to Jezebel, saying: 'Naboth has been stoned and is dead.' ¹⁵ When Jezebel heard that Naboth was stoned and was dead, she said to Ahab: 'Rise up, take possession of the vineyard of Naboth the Jezreelite, which he refused to give you for money, for Naboth is not alive, but dead.' ¹⁶ When Ahab heard that Naboth was dead, he rose up to go down to the vineyard of Naboth the Jezreelite, to take possession of it.

Symbolically, they send word to Jezebel, the archetype of greed, that the prophecies represented by Naboth, the dharma in human words, have been destroyed. When Lama Yeshe—a prominent transmitter of Tibetan Buddhism to the West—told a story of finding a broken Buddha statue in a Tibetan river, he surprised his audience by laughing so hard he almost fell out of his chair.[3] Did the Chinese occupiers really think they could destroy the dharma so easily?

Jezebel tells Ahab he now has power over the prophecies, over the dharma itself. Of course, this is a complete delusion, though it is seen in the more Constantinian political theologies and practices, when religion and government become too intertwined. More commonly, there is the idea that religion and spirituality are and should be subject to the laws of fashion and faddishness—how can you believe this *now*, in *this* day and age? As though that is relevant. Some would argue that my reading of the story of Elijah is just that, an attempt to water down the Bible's teachings or the Buddha's teachings to make them more palatable. I would rather be a fundamentalist or a Constantinian than a watered-down anything. But this is not about fashion. As with Jewish renewal, post-Evangelical and emerging Christianity, or convergent Quakerism, it is about connecting the old and the new, dharmic and Abrahamic insights, finding in the past the resources we need to move into the future.

Ahab doesn't wait around, he immediately persuades himself he is king over the prophecies, supreme governor, the wind of fashion that renders religious and spiritual values old-fashioned and obsolete. He 'rose up to go down'—a paradoxical turn of phrase emphasizing that Ahab thinks he is ascending to a higher level of kingship, but in reality the opposite is the case.

17 And the word of YHWH came to Elijah the Tishbite, saying...

Elijah reappears after a lengthy absence (unless the earlier unnamed prophet was him), and is back to being 'Elijah the Tishbite' after earlier being 'Elijah the prophet'. Is this a 'demotion'? It doesn't seem that way in context, though as we shall see he is a more 'normal' prophet than before. Is it an indication that the timescale is not linear? Possibly, though Ahab's new sense of entitlement seems to argue against this. However, there is an illusory quality to time, and progress on the spiritual path is experienced as more like a labyrinth than a straight line. Or is it simply a reminder that Elijah is still Elijah?

Being the prophet of Mount Carmel and Mount Horeb hasn't erased who he is. Rabbi Zusya needs to be more like Rabbi Zusya, not more like Moses. By trying to be what we are not, we can become as 'bland as Buddha', to echo George Mackay Brown's complaint, mentioned earlier.

[18] *'Rise up, go down to meet Ahab king of Israel, who is living in Samaria. He is in the vineyard of Naboth, where he has gone to take possession of it...'*

'Rise up, go down'—Elijah is told to go *down*, as though he has been on the mountain (which of course he has), communing with YHWH, in blissful samadhi like the arhat who has attained nirvana, and is told to go back to the valley, to Samaria. But Elijah rises up *by* going down, in contrast to Ahab, who rises up *to* go down, that is, he brings himself down by aiming high. We have seen that Samaria is the center of political power and of clinging to the delusions of selfhood, everything that is familiar and safe to Ahab, but ultimately it is samsara. It is also where Elijah's successor Elisha begins his ministry later. Like the Mahayana arhat who becomes a bodhisattva, Elijah leaves his state of bliss to re-enter the fray, but in reality this is a very short distance. Elijah gets there almost immediately; Ahab is still in the vineyard. It is not a *siddhi*, a magical power, but a natural ability of the mind to get to the heart of the matter; this natural ability has been obscured like a blue sky obscured by clouds, but Elijah's progress toward enlightenment is a clearing away of those clouds.

'...[19] You will tell him: YHWH says this: Have you killed, and also taken possession? And you also tell him: YHWH says this: In the place where dogs licked the blood of Naboth, dogs will lick yours, your blood.'

From the point of view of the later Hebrew prophets and the Tanakh as a whole, this is more like the 'normal' message of a prophet—social justice combined with fire and brimstone. Of course, this does raise issues of chronology, as with the traditional conflation of the Obadiah we met earlier with the author (or narrator) of the short book of Obadiah. But the words 'killed, and also taken possession' highlight a point in common between Elijah's concerns and the later message of social justice—the dharma, the word of being-itself, cannot really be destroyed, so the presumption to take possession of it is the more serious offense, because that is an attempt to tame and co-opt it for the purposes of political power. Rulers like Constantine and Ashoka have more in common with Ahab than Elijah.

[20] Ahab said to Elijah: 'Have you found me, my enemy?' He answered: 'I have found you, because you have given yourself over to do that which is evil in the sight of YHWH. [21] I will bring evil upon you, and will utterly sweep you away, and will cut off from Ahab every male descendent, those who are enslaved and those who are free in Israel. [22] I will make your house like the house of Jeroboam the son of Nebat, and like the house of Baasa the son of Ahijah, for the provocation with which you have provoked me, and because you have made Israel to sin.

'Have you found me, my enemy?' Earlier, Ahab asked Elijah 'Is it you, you troubler of Israel?', but these words have a similar flavor. This time, Elijah is much more blunt and to the point, and does not deny he is Ahab's enemy. There are hundreds of references to enemies in the Tanakh, particularly in the Psalms, and they can make for uncomfortable reading. But as Elias Hicks said, in the same spoken ministry quoted earlier: 'We need not look without for enemies or friends; for we shall not find them without. Our enemies are those of our own household: our own propensities and unruly desires are our greatest, and I may almost say, our alone enemies.'⁴ In short, Elijah is the enemy of what Ahab represents.

The phrase 'given yourself over to do that which is evil' is specifically a reference to Ahab's treatment of Naboth and what Naboth represents. Evil is about his treatment of the weak, like the shuttlebox that Mark Rowlands saw as the exemplar of evil, and it contrasts with God's preferential option for the poor. The connection between social justice and henotheism (at least) becomes clearer. Elijah doesn't repeat verbatim the words spoken to him earlier, but the spirit of the prophecy is the same. The prophet Muhammad said that divine revelation sometimes came in clear language, but at other times it sounded like a bell, which he had to work hard to 'translate'.⁵ A prophet is not a mindless automaton, a divine voice-recording, but someone who is one with the divine, however faintly this may be perceived. The language of Elijah's prophecy is one of punishment instigated by YHWH, but remember this is being-itself, so the language of karma is appropriate here. Ahab is the author of his own downfall, and so is Jezebel. Marx said capitalism contains the seeds of its own destruction—and this is true of the materialism fueled by dualism, self-absorption and self-entitlement that have been represented by Ahab and Jezebel. In the story of Elijah, their characters/archetypes are the ones that change and evolve the most, as though the arch-*kleshas* are the most chameleon-like, making them so difficult to uproot, transform, or apply the right antidote to. But Elijah also changes and evolves. As John Henry Newman said, 'to live is to change, and to be perfect is to have changed often.'⁶ There is a paradox here, but Elijah's change is teleological—changing toward enlightenment— while Ahab and Jezebel change in reaction to circumstances, fashions and even temptations, all as understood through the lens of karma.

According to Brueggemann, the malediction that follows refers to Ahab being cut off from a future dynasty. Furthermore, he says, 'the *destruction of one peasant* evokes *total dismissal of the dynasty.'*[7] We would be unsurprised if the killing of a king led to reprisals for a peasant's family, but this is the other way round. It is a *vivid demonstration* of God's preferential option for the poor. Earlier, we encountered the concept of spiritual poverty in relation to the widow of Zarephath—but the term 'poor in spirit' also appears in the Dead Sea Scrolls, where it is said the poor in spirit will defeat the hard of heart,[8] and in the Beatitudes, where it is said theirs is the Kingdom of Heaven.[9] Spiritually poor is not separated from materially poor; the Greek word for poor really means beggars, not people on a slightly lower income than their middle-class neighbors, so the poor in spirit can mean those who are so poor that even their spirits are crushed. The word translated 'spirit' can also be translated 'breath', so 'the poor in spirit' can mean 'those who beg for breath'—like George Floyd, for example.

The implications for the dynasty also remind us that karma can last for more than one lifetime, even to the third and fourth generation, as the Tanakh reminds us repeatedly. Because Ahab has 'made Israel to sin', the karma he created will last for many generations. Until now the widow of Zarephath and Obadiah are the only people who refer to sin, asking how *they* have sinned that their current circumstances have befallen them. However, in this case Ahab has *made Israel* to sin—the ones who struggle with God have been made to miss the mark, like a hunter who fails to make a clean kill but causes enough injury to result in a slow, painful death. The ones who struggle with God *have been made* to cause injury to God, to the ground of being, to the *alaya*, the storehouse consciousness from which our karma comes and to which our karma returns. We look at this again in the final chapter, but for now it is clear that this injury will last more than one generation.

^{23} *And of Jezebel YHWH also spoke, saying: The dogs will eat Jezebel in the moat of Jezreel.*

'The dogs will eat Jezebel in the moat of Jezreel'—again note that Jezreel means 'God sows', so this is a reference to karma, Jezebel reaping what she has sown, but not in a way that suggests she really is a distinct, unitary, permanent self. Again this is phenomenological, the karma is *experienced* as sown by El, the presiding deity and supreme being rather than being-itself, but actually it is sown by YHWH, by being-itself. Further to what we saw earlier, in the discussion of the meaning of Naboth's name, this chapter juxtaposes the phenomenological El with the ontological YHWH. They are not two beings—indeed, YHWH is not a being at all, but being-itself, the becoming possible of the impossible—but those who struggle with El are the true followers of YHWH. Although YHWH is more ontological and El or Elohim more experiential, yet in the Pentateuch it is YHWH who is written about in more anthropomorphic terms. This suggests that God is *experienced* as distant, paradoxically singular-yet-plural, forced to communicate through intermediaries, such as angels; whereas YHWH, being-itself, though apparently a more 'advanced' *ontological* concept, is nonetheless more *immanent*, because we all share in being.

^{24} *The one who dies and belongs to Ahab in the city, the dogs will eat, and the one who dies in the field, the birds of the air will eat.'*

There is an echo of the earlier verse: 'The one who escapes from the sword of Hazael, Jehu will kill, and the one who escapes from the sword of Jehu, Elisha will kill.' But it's strange that there's a reference to the one who belongs to Ahab, given that Elijah has already said there would be no *male* belonging to Ahab left, and the text doesn't say 'the woman who dies and belongs to Ahab'. Could it mean the *kleshas*, being parasitic, are effectively destroyed once they are abandoned? Or perhaps they need a (symbolically) male and female aspect to survive, because if they can't reproduce then their genes die out. The reference to the birds eating anyone who dies in the country is reminiscent of the Tibetan Buddhist practice of sky burial.

25 But there was nobody like Ahab, who gave himself over to do that which was evil in the sight of YHWH, stirred up by Jezebel his wife. 26 He did what was very abominable by following idols, in the same way that the Amorites did, whom YHWH cast out before the children of Israel.

The word 'abominable' is a ritual rather than an ethical one, but this is in the context of Ahab and Jezebel's treatment of Naboth, so the text is drawing a connection between the idolatrous religion to which Elijah is so hostile, and the materialism of Ahab and Jezebel. The link between idols and materialism is dramatically exposed, suggesting Biblical references to idol worship and the prohibition of idol worship are fundamentally about materialism, because money and wealth are the ultimate (false) idol, and the love of money is a root of all evil.[10] In Chaucer's 'Pardoner's Tale', it is this love of money (*cupiditas*) that leads to death.

The reference to the Amorites, the *kleshas* who are driven out *by* being-itself *before* the ones who struggle with El, suggests a going back, but not in the sense of the labyrinth where we can sometimes *seem* to be going back. Sometimes we can make the mistake of retracing our steps in the labyrinth in the mistaken belief it will help us progress, or of struggling to swim upstream in the hope it will get us to the sea of nirvana, what the Sufis call *fana*, the extinction of the self in God.

27 When Ahab heard those words, he tore his clothes and put sackcloth on his skin. He fasted, lay in sackcloth, and went softly.

*²⁸ And the word of YHWH came to Elijah the Tishbite, saying:
²⁹ 'Do you see how Ahab humbles himself before me? Because he
humbles himself before me, I will not bring the evil in his days, but
in his son's days I will bring the evil upon his house.'*

At the end of the last chapter and early in this one, Ahab is 'sullen
and dispirited', whereas now we read that he 'lay in sackcloth,
and went softly'. Possibly they would look the same from the
outside, but this is a real if limited transformation. There is
another fast, but with a very different motive. The spiritual path
is not about the external, but the internal, the motivation. The
road to heaven is paved with good intentions. However, Ahab's
materialistic mind does not grasp this, so he makes a point not
only of *practicing* the externals, but of *showing* he is practicing.
When you fast, says Jesus, fast in secret, anointing your head
and washing your face so people won't know you are fasting,
and then you will be rewarded.[11] In Buddhism, there are said to
be hidden yogis, people who hide their virtuous practices and
spiritual realizations, which often become known to others only
after the person has died.

However, YHWH still forgives him, in spite of the imperfect
nature of his regret. Even such limited regret and humility
wipes out large amounts of negative karma. Interestingly, the
emphasis of these verses is on how Ahab's humility is used as
a teaching for Elijah. He is not told to pass on this message; it
is for his own journey toward enlightenment, and since Elijah
represents you, the seeker, the questioner, this is for *your*
journey and *your* enlightenment.

The Lies of God (1 Kings 22)

Like the chapter before last, this chapter is concerned with war. It is possible to discern an implicit pacifism, a view that proportionality, or *jus in bello*, is never characteristic of war, however just the cause. But it is also possible to discern the view expounded in the Bhagavad Gita, that God is to be found where we are, where our karma has led us, even if that is on the battlefield. Elijah is again conspicuous by his absence here, unless he can be equated with Micaiah, which is possible. He seems to appear where we would expect Elijah to appear, and he is in some ways the same archetype, but appearing as a third-person minor character, allowing you to decenter yourself, to see your spiritual journey from a different point of view. Despite being prominent in this chapter, Ahab is not mentioned *by name* until after his death, and we see a frequent juxtaposition of 'Jehoshaphat' with 'the king of Israel'. Ahab is nonetheless the king of those who struggle with God, for now, while Jehoshaphat represents a kind of 'religious correctness', an intellectual assent to doctrine without a genuine transformation.

22 Three years went by without war between Aram and Israel.

There is an uneasy standoff between the one who struggles with God and the one subject to Ben-hadad and all he represents, but we know from Elijah's encounter with the still silence-sound on Mount Horeb that Hazael is waiting to be king of Aram; therefore Ben-hadad's days are numbered.

² In the third year, Jehoshaphat the king of Judah came down to the king of Israel, ³ and the king of Israel said to his servants: 'Do you know that Ramoth-gilead is ours, and yet we are not moving, not taking it back from the king of Aram?' ⁴ He said to Jehoshaphat:

'Will you go with me in battle to Ramoth-gilead?' Jehoshaphat said to the king of Israel: 'I am as you are, my people as your people, my horses as your horses.'

Jehoshaphat had a marriage alliance with Ahab, who had 'induced' him with material (and 'religiously correct') gifts of slaughtered sheep and oxen.[1] This is not quite a reunification of Israel and Judah, but an intriguing glimpse of that possibility. It represents the possibility that the raw struggle with God is not *necessarily* opposed to Jehoshaphat's religiosity, though the relationship between religion and spirituality is often an uneasy one. Some people find religion an obstacle to genuine spirituality, while others develop their spirituality gradually, through a regular engagement with religious practices and even rituals. Maybe these people have something to say to each other, if they can be empathic toward one another's hurts.

The reference to the third year echoes the beginning of the Elijah story, the reference to the third year of the drought. Ahab's reference to Gilead is a reference to Elijah's origin, the site of his nomadic encampment in a liminal space on the margins of Israel. Jehoshaphat does not regard these things as his own—this is consistent with the politics of *anatta* if not with the modern capitalist veneration of private property. His language echoes that of Ruth in the book of Ruth: 'your people will be my people and your God will be my God.'[2]

[5] Jehoshaphat also said to the king of Israel: 'Please ask for the word of YHWH today.'

This looks like an entirely genuine request, consistent with what we later read about Jehoshaphat. The Yahwist strand in the Pentateuch and (albeit less directly) in the Deuteronomic history does tend to be more pro-Judah than pro-Israel, so his reference to the word of YHWH fits what would be expected.

However, he seems to have in mind some sort of an oracle, as though he can ask YHWH a question and expect a direct answer. Sometimes meditating on a particular question can be the wrong thing to do. We need to listen to the silence, not try to manipulate it to our own preoccupations.

> [6] Then the king of Israel gathered four hundred prophets together and asked them: 'Shall I go into battle against Ramoth-gilead, or shall I stay at a distance?' They replied: 'Go up, because YHWH will deliver it into the hand of the king.' [7] But Jehoshaphat said: 'Still, is there not a prophet of YHWH here, that we might ask him?'

Ahab brings in four hundred prophets, ostensibly prophets of YHWH, but the number four hundred suggests they are the prophets of Asherah who didn't turn up at Mount Carmel, representing the *kleshas* of materialism, material comfort and self-preservation. Asherah and YHWH were sometimes seen as spouses, so I don't think Ahab is trying to trick Jehoshaphat. But Jehoshaphat is rightly suspicious that the prophets are saying what they think Ahab wants to hear, and perhaps Jehoshaphat too. Teresa of Avila said one characteristic of a *genuine* call, prophecy, or word from God is a certain element of surprise, not a gradual building up of what the ego wants to hear.[3] Moments of enlightenment, mini-*kenshos*, are similar. They are not just a confirmation but a surprise and yet, paradoxically, they are not a new revelation or worldview—mountains are mountains and rivers are rivers. They are what creative writers call an *inevitable* surprise.

> [8] The king of Israel said to Jehoshaphat: 'There is still one man by whom we may ask YHWH, Micaiah the son of Imlah, but I hate him, because he does not prophesy good concerning me, but evil.'

Jehoshaphat replied: 'Let not the king say so.' [9] *Then the king of Israel called an officer and said: 'Fetch quickly Micaiah the son of Imlah.'*

Is Micaiah Elijah? Not only does this fit with the psychological character of our reading, but it also fits with Ahab's statement that 'there is still *one* other' — presumably Elijah was not among the four hundred. Micaiah means 'who is like YHWH' (with or without a question mark), which, if it is an archetype, at least closely resembles Elijah, 'my God is YHWH'. The various Buddhas and Bodhisattvas of Mahayana Buddhism are ultimately all one, all representations (even avatars) of the one enlightened mind, the Buddha-nature, the Dharmakaya.

It becomes clear that Ahab really is the sort of king who encourages prophets to say what they think he wants to hear, to the apparent discomfort of Jehoshaphat. However, Ahab does at least recognize Jehoshaphat's counsel.

[10] *Now the king of Israel and Jehoshaphat the king of Judah sat on their thrones, arrayed in their robes, on a threshing-floor, at the entrance of the gate of Samaria, and all the prophets prophesied before them.*

The threshing-floor is a theme in the Tanakh. It is the site of David's altar, for example, which would eventually be the site of the Jerusalem temple, and it is where Ruth revealed to Boaz that he was her kinsman-redeemer,[4] possibly emphasizing the earlier echoing of Ruth in this chapter. Yet the scene is one of royal pomp — thrones and robes — and the prophets are at the service of political power. Clearly something is wrong.

[11] *Zedekiah the son of Chenaanah made him horns of iron and said: 'YHWH says this: With these you will gore the Arameans, until*

*they are consumed.' *[12]* And all the prophets prophesied the same thing, saying: 'Go up to Ramoth-gilead and prosper; for YHWH will deliver it into the hand of the king.'*

There is something comical about the idea that an army can be destroyed with a pair of horns. The *kleshas* can't be uprooted or transformed in a casual way. It requires trust, which can be seen here, but this is a casual one-off act of optimism, when what is needed is a real commitment. It is the work of becoming enlightened, which is the pearl of great price, for which we must be ready to sell everything in order to purchase just that one thing — and that one thing may be just the next step, a glimpse of the next signpost, not even the destination itself.

[13] The messenger that went to fetch Micaiah said to him: 'With one mouth the prophets speak good words to the king. Please let your word be like their word, and speak what is good.' [14] Micaiah said: 'As YHWH lives, what YHWH says to me, that I will speak.' [15] When he had come to the king, the king said to him: 'Micaiah, shall we go into battle against Ramoth-gilead, or shall we stay at a distance?' He answered him: 'Go up and prosper, and YHWH will deliver it into the hand of the king.' [16] The king said unto him: 'How many times shall I charge you to speak nothing to me but the truth in the name of YHWH?'

The ethos of saying what the king wants to hear is made even more explicit by the messenger. As earlier, the word translated 'messenger' is the same word that is translated as 'angel'. Micaiah rejects this ethos of conformity, but then he seems to change his mind. However, could it be the king's lack of faith that is his downfall? He does not believe he is worthy of a good prophecy — his karma has instilled in him a kind of remorse, but not a metanoia. It is his own judgement of himself that will come to fruition.

[17] He said: 'I saw all Israel scattered on the mountains, like sheep without a shepherd, and YHWH said: They have no master. Let each one of them return to their house in peace.' [18] The king of Israel said to Jehoshaphat: 'Did I not tell you that he would not prophesy good concerning me, but evil?'

From Micaiah's point of view there is something alarming about sheep without a shepherd, but from YHWH's point of view it is the natural order of things that they not have a master, meaning they can 'return to their house in peace'. The politics of *anatta* are not hierarchical. There are multiple layers here: to be enlightened, even to realize non-duality, means not to be mastered by one's own mind, or by social expectations. Even the smallest glimpse of enlightenment is experienced as a homecoming, an end to struggling upstream in search of the sea, 'a dwelling in a natural state, and a spontaneous abiding', as the Buddhist philosopher Asanga said of equanimity.[5]

Ahab seems oddly satisfied, as though this is in line with what he expected. It is noteworthy that the text does not imply criticism of Micaiah for his initial prophecy, either for the reason suggested earlier—that Ahab's lack of faith makes him unable to accept the first prophecy—or because the second prophecy is the one that Ahab accepts, or even because he is an agent of the 'lying' spirit we are about to encounter.

[19] Micaiah said: 'Therefore listen to the word of YHWH. I saw YHWH sitting on his throne, and all the host of heaven standing beside him on his right hand and on his left. [20] And YHWH said: Who will entice Ahab to go to Ramoth-gilead, so that he will fall there? One said: In this way; and another said: In that way. [21] A spirit came out and stood before YHWH and said: I will entice him. [22] And YHWH asked: How? The spirit said: I will go out and be a lying spirit in the mouth of all his prophets. And YHWH said: You will entice him, and will also succeed. Go out, and do so. [23] Now

therefore, YHWH has put a lying spirit in the mouth of all these your prophets, and YHWH has spoken evil concerning you.'

This may be one of the strangest passages in the Bible, because it evokes a scenario of YHWH deliberately misleading human beings by putting a lying spirit in the mouths of the prophets. It is a very Yahwist passage—the word YHWH is used repeatedly. The prophets all speak in the name of YHWH, not another deity or demonic force, and yet they lie. This is historically intelligible, but very strange in this context, because it suggests a prophecy can be from God and yet be false. For this reason, it has caused plenty of debate. There is a non-duality of good and evil represented here, which is a difficult concept to convey. In Genesis, the fall occurred when Adam and Eve ate the fruit of the tree of the knowledge of good and evil[6]—in other words, when they separated good from evil. Deutero-Isaiah writes: 'I am YHWH, and there is none else. I form the light, and create darkness, I make peace, and create evil. I am YHWH, that does all these things.'[7] This non-dual understanding of the ground of being, which encompasses good and evil, truth and lies, is memorably echoed by Ahmad Ghazali when he claims that anyone who does not learn divine unity from Satan is an infidel,[8] and Meister Eckhart honors those who 'have given up all good works...since in the eternal Word is neither bad nor good', commenting 'therefore they are absolutely empty'[9], empty in Buddhist terms, that is.

Any of this can be used as an excuse for following evil and eschewing good, but Rumi's field is beyond *ideas* of right and wrong, and it is there we can meet and discuss and commune. Hence the nature of Kierkegaard's distinction between the ethical and the religious—the one is a *transformation* of the other, not a simple lack.

There is also a hint that truth is more than simple facticity. This is echoed in the Gospels, where Jesus says he will not go to the festival, but later goes in secret, at night, so he cannot be seen.[10] In the Lotus Sutra (composed several centuries after the Buddha), the Buddha praises the father who enticed his children to leave a burning building by telling them there were numerous toy carts outside, even though there was only one such cart, in which the children were taken to safety. This is seen as an allegory for enticing people into the one buddha-vehicle by teaching them about the three vehicles: hearer, solitary realizer and bodhisattva.[11] To tell the truth and avoid lies is a core precept for Buddhists, just as it is a core testimony for Quakers, but these passages suggest something more to truth than facticity. When Solzhenitsyn said 'one word of truth outweighs the world', he put forward a positive conception of truth rather than a negative one that stops at the mere avoidance of lies.

[24] *Zedekiah the son of Chenaanah came near to Micaiah and struck him on the cheek, then said: 'Which way did the spirit of YHWH go from me to speak to you?'* [25] *Micaiah said: 'You will see on that day when you go into an inner chamber to hide yourself.'*

Both references to Zedekiah in this chapter make him seem like a court jester among the prophets, but there is something about his theatrics that also makes him seem less than trustworthy. It is reminiscent of prophets like Hosea and Ezekiel, and some Zen masters and teachers of 'crazy wisdom' who do something to shock their pupils into awareness, yet the same thing done with a different motivation could be theatrical for the sake of being theatrical, and may even be harmful, as is the case here.

Zedekiah is also the name of the last king of Judah before the Babylonian exile—perhaps his role here is symbolic, a situating of the Elijah narrative within that context. The name means 'righteousness of YHWH' or 'justice of YHWH' (righteousness and justice being the same thing in Hebrew, as in many other languages), and the prophesied event is not mentioned elsewhere in the book of Kings or the rest of the Tanakh, adding support to a symbolic reading within the context of the Babylonian exile, an exilic or post-exilic perspective on pre-exilic Israel. And it was that exile which, above all else, transformed the Jewish faith from a henotheistic to a monotheistic one, expanding the possibility for a non-dual understanding of YHWH as the ground of being, as being-itself.

The reference to an inner chamber is somewhat enigmatic; it is what Ben-hadad fled to earlier, and there also seems to be some Hebrew wordplay here (inner chamber is *heder beheder*). There is no record of this prophecy coming to pass, but it is when we look deeply into ourselves that we discover the truth about ourselves, and this can be experienced as a slap on the cheek, a shock we want to hide from.

> [26] *The king of Israel said: 'Take Micaiah and carry him back to Amon the governor of the city, and to Joash the king's son,* [27] *and say: The king says this: Put this man in the prison, and feed him with the bread and water of oppression, until I return in peace.'*

Despite his instruction to speak only the truth, Ahab punishes Micaiah for doing so. While the ego claims to want to know the truth, it does so assuming it can control the truth. Micaiah is fed with 'the bread and water of oppression', seemingly an expression referring to a prison diet, but it also highlights the oppressive nature of the regime, and the oppressive nature of the ego. A word of surprise can shake the ego and make it revert to previous patterns. To hear the surprising word of enlightenment, we need to be ready, genuinely ready, to hear what may surprise us.

> [28] *Micaiah said: 'If you return at all in peace, YHWH has not spoken by me.' And he said: 'Listen you peoples, all of you.'*

The enlightened mind represented by Micaiah knows it will ultimately prevail, everywhere, among all peoples, and that the *kleshas* represented by Ahab—although he is unnamed here— are living on borrowed time and ruling with an authority that is not their own, that is illusory.

> [29] *So the king of Israel and Jehoshaphat the king of Judah went up to Ramoth-gilead.*

Strangely, despite his earlier insistence on hearing from the prophets of YHWH, Jehoshaphat goes along with Ahab's desire to go into battle, and with his plan. Perhaps his desire to consult the prophets was motivated principally (if not exclusively) by 'religious correctness'. We have seen that in Theravada Buddhism it is said one cannot even attain the stage of stream-enterer (*sotapanna*, the first step on the irreversible road to *nibbana*, or nirvana) without transcending the attachment to religious rituals and ceremonies. Jehoshaphat does not seem to have reached this stage—indeed, he *represents* a stage that is prior to this one.

> [30] *The king of Israel said to Jehoshaphat: 'I will disguise myself and go into the battle, but you put on your robes.' The king of Israel disguised himself and went into the battle.* [31] *Now the king of Aram had given this command to the thirty-two captains of his chariots: 'Do not fight with the small or the great, but only with the king of Israel.'* [32] *When the captains of the chariots saw Jehoshaphat they said: 'Surely that is the king of Israel'. They turned aside to fight against him, and Jehoshaphat cried out.* [33] *When the captains of the chariots saw it was not the king of Israel, they turned back from pursuing him.* [34] *A certain man drew his bow right back, and struck the king of Israel between the lower armor and the breastplate, at which he said to the driver of his chariot: 'Turn round and carry me out of here, because I am seriously wounded.'*

35 The battle became fiercer that day, and the king was stood up in his chariot facing the Arameans. He died at evening, and the blood ran out of the wound into the bottom of the chariot. 36 A cry went throughout the army as the sun went down, saying: 'Everyone to their own city and their own country.' 37 So the king died and was brought to Samaria, and they buried the king in Samaria.

When Ben-hadad first appeared in the story, he had thirty-two kings with him. Now, they are thirty-two 'captains of his chariots'. He has become more autocratic, not in spite of his earlier defeats but because of them, because it is the lesser *kleshas* that are uprooted first. They have not been transformed into something more positive. Earlier, they were replaced by clones of Ben-hadad, and now they are demoted into auxiliaries of the *klesha* represented by him, that is anger, self-importance and sense of entitlement.

Ahab's disguise can be compared with the prophet's headband. He tries to disguise himself, but in reality he cannot. It is not entirely clear if the archer fired the arrow at random, as some translations suggest, or if the bow was drawn fully back in order to give the arrow more speed and distance. But there is a sense of inevitability about what happens. His weak spot is found, in the same way that karmic causes always have karmic effects. His death and the end of the battle both occur at the time of the evening prayer, when daytime consciousness intermingles with nighttime consciousness, but he does not seem to have any last-minute conversion. Instead, he is taken back to samsara, and buried there.

38 They washed the chariot by the pool of Samaria, and the dogs licked up his blood. The prostitutes also washed themselves there, according to the word of YHWH which he spoke.

There is no earlier reference to the prostitutes, so the end of this verse is puzzling, and has led to centuries of inconclusive commentary. But the dogs licking the blood of Ahab has already been prophesied by Elijah. The dogs may represent the *nafs* — the lower self in Sufism — but they and the prostitutes are agents of being-itself. They participate in divine being as surely as do kings and prophets. In each one of us there is an Elijah and an Ahab, a dog and a prostitute. Earlier we asked if the *kleshas* were to be rooted out and destroyed, or transformed and redeemed. Now we see that the *kleshas* represented by Ahab need to be removed, and it is *by* being removed that they *are* transformed, transformed into something useful — water for drinking and washing. Rumi compares himself to a piece of dung, not in a self-hating way, but asking that the sunlight might shine on him and dry him out, so he can be used as fuel to provide warmth and light in a bathhouse.[12] Water and dung may seem mundane, banal, but they have a reality to them that the *kleshas* do not.

³⁹ Now the rest of the acts of Ahab and all that he did, the ivory house and all the cities that he built, are they not written in the book of the chronicles of the kings of Israel? ⁴⁰ So Ahab slept with his fathers, and Ahaziah his son reigned in his place.

The reference to the ivory house and the cities that he built is interesting. He seems like the sort of a dictator (a Franco or a Pinochet) who is praised in some quarters for improving the economy and bringing stability to the country, as though these things excuse or mitigate his human rights record. But things are viewed differently from the viewpoint of the politics of *anatta*, where materialism is seen to be a false idol, and the love of money to result only in death. Motivation is more important than material achievement, whatever the 'hard-headed' materialists might claim.

[41] Jehoshaphat the son of Asa began to reign over Judah in the fourth year of Ahab the king of Israel. [42] Jehoshaphat was thirty-five years old when he began to reign, and he reigned for twenty-five years in Jerusalem. His mother's name was Azubah the daughter of Shilhi. [43] He walked wholly in the way of Asa his father. He did not turn aside from it, but did what was right in the eyes of YHWH. [44] Indeed, the high places were not taken away, and the people still sacrificed and offered incense in the high places. [45] Jehoshaphat made peace with the king of Israel. [46] Now the rest of the acts of Jehoshaphat, and his strength that he showed and how he made war, are they not written in the book of the chronicles of the kings of Judah? [47] He expelled from the land the remnant of temple prostitutes that remained in the days of his father Asa. [48] There was no king in Edom: a deputy was king. [49] Jehoshaphat made ships of Tarshish to go to Ophir for gold, but they did not go, because the ships were broken up in the port of Ezion-geber. [50] Then Ahaziah the son of Ahab said to Jehoshaphat: 'Let my servants go with your servants in the ships.' But Jehoshaphat would not. [51] Jehoshaphat slept with his fathers, and was buried with his fathers in the city of David his father, and Jehoram his son reigned in his place. [52] Ahaziah the son of Ahab began to reign over Israel in Samaria in the seventeenth year of Jehoshaphat the king of Judah, and he reigned over Israel for two years. [53] He did what was evil in the sight of YHWH, and walked in the way of his father, in the way of his mother, and in the way of Jeroboam the son of Nebat, and in that way he made Israel to sin. [54] He served Baal and worshipped him, and provoked YHWH the God of Israel in all the same ways that his father had done.

Jehoshaphat is contrasted with Ahab. As we saw earlier, Jehoshaphat represents a kind of 'religious correctness', an intellectual assent to doctrine without a genuine transformation, metanoia, realization, enlightenment. It is not clear if the first word in verse 44 should be translated 'indeed' (as here), implying that Jehoshaphat had rightly maintained the high places where people worshipped YHWH; or 'however' (the more common translation), implying they were used for the worship of other deities and that this was a blot on Jehoshaphat's record. I think it is a deliberate ambiguity, our reaction telling us something about our own minds. Do we view YHWH as censorious, and spiritual practice as something that should be done 'correctly', or is it about an inner 'burning' that transcends attachment and aversion to rituals and ceremonies?

Ahab is dead, but the *klesha* has not been uprooted for good. The struggle must continue year after year, generation after generation, lifetime after lifetime. Yet it will end, because ultimately there is only one thing that is real, and it is not a thing: it is Buddha-nature, being-itself, the ground of being, YHWH. It will end because the ground of being is the becoming possible of the impossible.

This is the end of the book of 1 Kings, but the story of Elijah continues into the beginning of 2 Kings. In Jewish tradition, they are both parts of one book, the book of Kings; the division into 1 Kings and 2 Kings has more to do with later Christian tradition. That said, we cannot be sure if they were originally a single manuscript, or two, or possibly more. We will see at the end of the next chapter that this uncertainty has an influence on how we read the text.

The Labyrinth and the Mandala (2 Kings 1)

Once again, fire is an important theme in this chapter, and it is worth reminding ourselves of the tension in this theme: it is an important pro-Cyrus symbol of late exilic and post-exilic politics, and yet Elijah on Mount Horeb discovered 'YHWH was not in the fire'.

1 Moab rebelled against Israel after the death of Ahab.

That Israel is the one to be rebelled against is an interesting assumption, but this is after the death of Ahab, so it seems as though Moab had been waiting for a moment of weakness.

2 Ahaziah fell down through the lattice in his upper chamber that was in Samaria, and he became sick. He sent messengers and said to them: 'Go, ask Baal-zebub the God of Ekron whether I will recover from this sickness.'

The 'upper chamber' might suggest an allusion to the 'inner chamber' of the last chapter, but it is a different Hebrew word. When Elijah is with the widow of Zarephath, he also is in an 'upper chamber'—the Hebrew there is *ha'aliyah*, but here it is *ba'aliyah*, as though there is deliberate punning going on, using the name of Baal. Traditionally the word *aliyah* is used for the act of 'going up' to read the Torah in the synagogue, and more recently it also has the Zionist meaning of migration to Israel. If Elijah's upper chamber symbolizes his merit, and inviting the widow's son into his chamber symbolizes the sharing of merit, then the king's falling from his upper chamber symbolizes the exhaustion of his merit—he has no good karma left for himself or to share with others, and this is later confirmed by his having no son to inherit his throne.

The instruction to go to Baal-zebub adds support to the idea that this is wordplay. Baal-zebul (Lord Prince or Lord of Princes) is changed to Baal-zebub, Lord of the Flies, the second pun involving the name of Baal in this one verse. This sort of punning in the Biblical text undermines certain (mainly Evangelical) theories of Biblical inspiration, which see the Bible unproblematically as a clear communication from God to human beings, and as having a 'plain meaning'. This view is sometimes attributed to the leaders of the Reformation, but Martin Luther said 'no man sees one iota in the Scriptures, but he that hath the Spirit of God',[1] a view that seems closer to Quakerism than modern-day Evangelicalism. The 'plain meaning' view is supposed to be a Christian one, but it seems a long way from what Richard Rohr calls the Jesus hermeneutic: for example, emphasizing *experience* of God and humanity, emphasizing positive commandments to love, flouting allegedly sacred taboos, using the Bible to defend and include people, not to punish or shame them.[2]

Again, the king sends *malakim*, messengers, or angels. There seems to be a certain fatalism in his question—not 'what should I do' or 'what should my doctor do' but 'whether I will recover'. Sometimes in our modern world we go to the opposite extreme, to a 'functional atheism', the attitude that it all depends on me. Wisdom lies in a middle way here. 'I will recover' translates the Hebrew *'ehyeh'*, also used by God in the burning bush, saying *ehyeh asher ehyeh*, I am what I am, I am who is, I am being-itself. Ahaziah is asking whether he will be, so it is not too great a stretch to suggest he is asking if he will participate in being-itself.

We have already encountered the phrase 'in Samaria' and its significance. It is the center of political power, where those in power feel comfortable and safe, but really it is samsara, the place of clinging to the delusions of selfhood.

³ But an angel of YHWH said to Elijah the Tishbite: 'Rise up, go up to meet the messengers of the king of Samaria and say to them: Is it because there is no God in Israel that you are going to ask Baal-zebub the God of Ekron...?'

Again he is 'Elijah the Tishbite' rather than 'Elijah the prophet'. Earlier, we considered the possibility that this indicated a 'demotion', or a non-linearity in the timescale emphasizing the illusory quality of time, or a simple reminder that Elijah is still Elijah, the nomad from the liminal margins of the land of Israel. He is told to 'rise up', as though he has been asleep, not yet awakened, not yet enlightened, or as though he is down emotionally, like the time he prayed he might die. As with Jezebel's messenger of death and the angel who provided Elijah with cake and water, there is a repetition of *malak/malakim*, emphasizing the contrast between messengers of YHWH and the messengers of political power, of Ahaziah who represents Ahab's legacy, the legacy of what Ahab represents, but has no legacy of his own, as we see later.

The question 'Is it because there is no God in Israel...?' again highlights the henotheistic theme of the Elijah story. Even though it is close to the end and there have been glimpses of monotheism, even of non-duality, the henotheistic strand is still there. It is something to be transcended, built upon, not thrown away as though dualistically opposed to 'true' non-duality, or even monotheism.

'...⁴ Now therefore YHWH says this: You will not come down from the bed to which you have gone up, but will surely die.' And Elijah departed.

This is a response to Ahaziah's fatalism, as well as his action of asking Baal-zebub. Note that the decalogue does not *explicitly* forbid the asking of questions to other Gods, but to 'having' them 'before' or 'besides' God, or to 'worshipping' them. This is an indirect hint then, that asking for help is a form of worship, not a selfish act we should somehow feel ashamed of. The English word 'pray' comes from the French 'prier', to ask—it involves a recognition of our own limitations, our dependence on a higher power, whether that be a supreme being (experienced as El, for example) or the ground of being, being-itself (YHWH). This recognition is not something that scares us into worship, or that inspires us to worship. This recognition *is* worship.

[5] *The messengers returned to him, and he asked them: 'Why have you returned?'*

The messengers return to the king rather than carrying out their task, but the contrast is not so absolute—they believe themselves to be, and experience themselves as, messengers of political power, but in reality, ontologically, they are messengers of YHWH, they are *malakim*, angels. Maybe they equate YHWH with Baal-zebub, or maybe the king has given ambiguous instructions such as 'ask the God', assuming they know what he means. When discussing other religions, Buddhists sometimes conflate 'God' with 'a creator God', which makes it harder to appreciate the full Buddhist significance of the ground of being, and to recognize what Buddhism has in common with other religions. To say God is a creator is one thing, but to import this into a *definition* of God confuses being-itself with *a* being. Buddhist teacher Alan Wallace writes that 'Vajrayana Buddhist cosmogony, specifically as presented in the Atiyoga tradition of Indo-Tibetan Buddhism, which presents itself as the culmination of all Buddhist teachings, reveals a theory of a transcendent ground of being and a process of creation that bear remarkable similarities with views presented in Vedānta and Neoplatonic Western Christian theories of creation.' He expands on those Western theories with a brief discussion of John Scotus Eriugena, who argued that 'the divine nothingness, which is ontologically prior to the very categories of existence and nonexistence, manifests in the phenomenal world', so 'the whole of creation can be called a theophany, or divine appearance, and nothing could exist apart from that divine nature, for it is the essence of all that is.' Similarly, Wallace goes on to say, from the Vajrayana perspective already alluded to, 'the primordial Buddha whose nature is identical with the *tathāgatagarbha* [Buddha-nature] within each sentient being, is the ultimate ground of *saṃsāra* and *nirvāṇa*; and the entire universe consists of nothing other than displays of this infinite, radiant, empty awareness.'[3]

> [6] *They said to him: 'A man came up to meet us, and he said to us: Go, return to the king who sent you and say to him: YHWH says this: Is it because there is no God in Israel that you are sending to ask Baal-zebub the God of Ekron? Therefore, you will not come down from the bed to which you have gone up, but will surely die.'*

The theme of stylistic repetition is explored earlier, but the repetition here is slightly different, because the text shows the angel telling Elijah what to say, and the messengers repeating what Elijah has said, but it does not recount Elijah actually saying this to the messengers. Elijah becomes temporarily insignificant, a link in the chain rather than the larger-than-life heroic figure he has been, and will be again. But when we awaken from the illusion of our own separateness, to use Thich Nhat Hanh's words, then we realize that the link is of the same substance as the chain, that a drop of water is of the same substance as the ocean. I am a part of the universe, and so are you. In their book *The New Monasticism*, Rory McEntee and Adam Bucko write:

There was a hermit who lived in the Sahara in Algeria, a Christian hermit, Charles de Foucauld. He lived as a hermit among Muslims and throughout his lifetime never found any disciples. One day he was killed by a band of marauders. By all accounts he was a failure according to any conventional measurement of the world. Years after he died, people were inspired by his writings and vision and gathered and prayed to him, forming the Little Brothers of Jesus. So you never know how it will come into being. It was the same with Abhishiktananda — it's now that we can appreciate him. This is important to ponder. Parker Palmer said that there are thousands of ways of being *almost* yourself. If you sway to the enticements of society, or a need for relevancy, then you move only further from your truth.[4]

I think this is a concrete example of what Jesus meant when he said that unless a grain of wheat falls to the ground and dies, it remains alone,[5] and what Thomas Merton meant when he said the one thing we should avoid at all costs is success.[6] Zen master Zengetsu put it this way: 'Live with cause and leave results to the great law of the universe.'[7] And what is the great law of the universe if it is not the gentle whisper, the still silence-sound Elijah heard on Mount Horeb?

> [7] He said to them: 'What kind of man was he that came up to meet you, and told you these words?' [8] They answered him: 'He was a hairy man, with a leather waist-cloth wrapped around his waist.' And he said: 'It is Elijah the Tishbite.'

The king is concerned with the 'sort of man' who said these things — he is not going to take it from just anyone. However, the fact that the man knew what the messengers were doing and what Ahaziah's question was, is significant. The messengers hadn't asked Elijah who he was, or, if they had, he hadn't told them. But the short description is enough—it is as though the king already knew on some level that it was Elijah. Elijah is wearing a leather waist-cloth around his waist. More likely this means the skin of a dead animal he had found somewhere, and it acts as a reference to his earlier act of wrapping his cloak around his waist, and of Ben-hadad's servants wrapping sackcloth around their waists. The Buddha's followers stitched together bits of cloth they found in charnel grounds, and these evolved into the monastic robes that are commonly seen in Buddhist countries today. Simplicity of dress is a common spiritual practice that serves as a protest against certain forms of social snobbery and ostentation, against the wastefulness and exploitation of the fashion industry, as well as a reminder to focus inwardly.[8]

⁹ Then the king sent to him a captain of fifty, with his fifty. He went up to Elijah, who sat on the top of the hill. He spoke to him: 'Man of God, the king has said: Come down.' ¹⁰ Elijah answered the captain of fifty: 'If I am a man of God, let fire come down from heaven and consume you and your fifty.' And there came down fire from heaven, and it consumed him and his fifty. ¹¹ The king sent to him another captain of fifty with his fifty, who answered and said to him: 'Man of God, the king has said this: Come down quickly.' ¹² Elijah answered and said to them: 'If I am a man of God, let fire come down from heaven and consume you and your fifty.' And the fire of God came down from heaven and consumed him and his fifty.

Two groups of fifty people are consumed, destroyed—again this seems very casual with regard to the killing of large numbers of people, not least because they are not even the ones who are at fault. But read symbolically, they are *kleshas* related to arrogance, seen in the assumption that a prophet of YHWH is at their beck and call, that enlightenment will come when it is convenient for us, as in the story of the Dalai Lama weeping when someone asked him for the easiest, quickest and cheapest way to enlightenment. The cheapest way demands we sell everything we have to afford it, because it is the pearl of great price. The easiest way is too difficult for the high achievers, but well within the capacity of a little child. But there is no quickest way, for it comes when we least expect it, on the way home from a meditation retreat, when the bottom falls out of a pail of water.[9]

There is also a significance to Elijah sitting on top of a hill, a place of safety like Mount Carmel, so he can only come down voluntarily and not be forced. He is addressed as man of *Elohim*, which can mean God or the Gods. The blurred distinction in Hebrew between God and Gods has already been discussed. In this passage, Elijah also says *Elohim*, but there is a clear contrast between his notion of *Elohim* and that of the messengers. For them, *Elohim* is controllable; Elijah shows that is not the case.

The theme of fire, which is so important in the story of Elijah, appears again. The *kleshas* are destroyed by fire. Even *after* discovering YHWH was not in the fire, fire still symbolizes YHWH's power, hence Elijah's progress toward enlightenment not being perfectly linear but more like a *labyrinth*. According to the Tibetan Buddhist discipline of *salam*, paths and grounds, only some paths are uninterrupted and irreversible. In Herman Hesse's novel *Siddhartha*, the central character's journey to enlightenment also appears to go back and forward, but this is only from a certain perspective, as we see by the end of the novel. The mandala looks different from the center.

There is more repetition here, though the second captain is if anything more presumptuous. He knows what happened to the first group, so he tries to counter this with a stronger demonstration of *political* authority: he 'answered', as though in defiance of Elijah's previous demonstration of power, 'and said to him: The king has said *this*,' a reminder that the king would expect unthinking obedience: 'Come down *quickly!*' But the effect is the same.

The first time, Elijah addresses the captain only, the second time he answers 'them', the group. The first time, fire from heaven destroys them, the second time it is the fire of God — *Elohim* — from heaven. Remember that the word for heaven is the same as the word for sky, so we could say that the first fire is from the sky and the second fire is from heaven. In Buddhist language, the first set of *kleshas* are destroyed by conventional means and the second by means of the ultimate. Elijah has got to the point in his meditation practice where a distraction can appear and be immediately destroyed as though by fire from the sky, and fifty distractions can appear and be immediately destroyed as though by the fire of God from heaven.

[13] *The king sent the captain of a third fifty with his fifty. The third captain of fifty went up, came before Elijah, fell on his knees and begged him: 'Man of God, please let my life and the life of these fifty, your servants, be precious in your sight.* [14] *There came down fire from heaven, and it consumed the two former captains of fifty with their fifties, but now let my life be precious in your sight.'* [15] *And the angel of YHWH said to Elijah: 'Go down with him. Do not be afraid of him.'*

Once more, things are done in threes, like the healing of the widow of Zarephath's son and the pouring of water around the altar on Mount Carmel. The third group does not make the same assumption as the first two; their captain shows humility. It might be self-preservation, so it is not a perfect humility, but it is nonetheless commendable and implicitly commended. He doesn't simply say 'man of *Elohim*' as a title, but recognizes that Elijah really is a representative of *Elohim* — though not of YHWH the ground of being — and that his life and the lives of his fifty are subject to something higher and wider. Again, there is a lot of fatalism here, but this is arguably the right time for fatalism, just as there is a wrong time for fatalism, which was exemplified in Ahaziah's initial reaction to his sickness.

The captain shows that he knows what happened before, confirming that the second captain had also known it. He repeats the plea 'let my life be precious in your sight'. It is interesting that *Elijah* is told not to be afraid of *him*, as though the fire from heaven was called because of *Elijah's* fear. Elijah seems unsure what to do with this gentle pleading—he hasn't entirely reached the point in his meditation practice where he is undistracted by virtuous thoughts. As any meditation teacher will tell you, being distracted by virtuous thoughts is still being distracted.

He rose up and went down with him to the king. [16] He said to him: 'Because you have sent messengers to ask Baal-zebub the God of Ekron, YHWH says this: Is it because there is no God in Israel whose word you can ask for? Therefore, you will not come down from the bed to which you have gone up, but will surely die.'

After all that, what happens is merely what had been foreshadowed earlier, both in the word of YHWH to Elijah, and in the king's request (or demand) to Elijah to come. There is no new proposition and no new revelation. Mountains are mountains and rivers are rivers, but Ahaziah doesn't understand what this means.

[17] So he died according to the word of YHWH which Elijah had spoken. And Jehoram began to reign in his place in the second year of Jehoram the son of Jehoshaphat king of Judah, because he had no son. [18] Now the rest of the acts of Ahaziah and all that he did, are they not written in the book of the chronicles of the kings of Israel?

The phrase 'he died *according to*' could mean he died *because of*, or *as predicted by*. The fact he has no heir is significant— Ahab had one, but Ahaziah does not. This confirms what we saw earlier, that he has no merit to pass on, no legacy of his own, that his good karma has been exhausted. The final verse is a repetition, at least stylistically, of the end of 1 Kings, which suggests business as usual. If 1 Kings and 2 Kings were originally separate manuscripts (which cannot be ruled out), then this would have been an important point for the author to make. The fact that we don't know, that we are uncertain about the original manuscripts, even to the extent of whether this is one book or more, highlights the importance of humility in reading the text. The third captain of fifty demonstrates this humility, not just on his own behalf but also on behalf of his fifty. Bringing this humility to the text adds something to the dictum with which this book began, 'the more interpretations the better'. It is not simply that we have the right to interpret the meaning for ourselves, but that a diversity of interpretations is a blessing, a *barakah*, as Muslims say of the diversity of interpretations in Islamic law.

Enlightenment (2 Kings 2:1–13a)

This is a very Yahwist passage—there are nine references to YHWH in the first six verses. Elijah and Elisha journey from Gilgal to Bethel to Jericho to the Jordan. The groups of prophets mirror the groups of soldiers in the last chapter—the first two groups say the same thing and are told to be silent, whereas the third group (also of fifty) actually does remain silent. The instruction to be silent is significant in itself, a reminder not to speak of that which cannot be put into words.

The story of Elijah ends with very Zoroastrian imagery. The chariots of fire are a Zoroastrian theme, which adds support to a post-exilic or late exilic dating of the text, or at least this part of it. The author is siding with the Persians against the Babylonians—in which case it is not necessarily post-exilic but reflects a period in which 'the signs of the times' point to the possibility that the exile is coming to an end. By extension, the author is also siding with the Persian religion against the Babylonian one, the former being instrumental in the development of Jewish monotheism and other tenets of post-exilic Judaism. On the dating of the text, however, the insistence that there can be only one God in Israel could be a challenge to the religious practices of those who had not been deported, who continued to practice (or at least were accused of practicing) a henotheistic worship of YHWH as part of a larger pantheon.

2 *When YHWH would take up Elijah by a whirlwind into heaven, Elijah went with Elisha from Gilgal.*

The text says 'when YHWH would take up Elijah by a whirlwind into heaven', as though it is obvious that this is going to happen. The text emphasizes it is by a whirlwind, not by the chariots of fire, as is often believed. YHWH is not in the fire, but neither is

YHWH in the wind. Despite the Yahwist language there is still an Elohist distance between Elijah and God. However, Elijah's enlightenment is about to happen, and it will be sudden, though not unexpected. He has become a stream-enterer, he is on the path of no return. He has not found enlightenment by seeking, yet he would not have found it had he not been a seeker.

The name Gilgal means a circle of stones, which could be an allusion to polytheistic worship, or to the Israelites' camp after they crossed the Jordan under the leadership of Joshua, or a number of other things. Whatever its significance, Elijah and Elisha are on their way *from* there.

> [2] *And Elijah said to Elisha: 'Please wait here, because YHWH has sent me as far as Bethel.' Elisha said: 'As YHWH lives and as your soul lives, I will not leave you.' So they went down to Bethel.*

They are on their way *to* Bethel, *Beth El*, the house of God. This is significant because it is the place where Jacob slept and had the dream of the ladder with angels ascending and descending. An angel is the embodiment of a *task*, so the ascending and descending represent the different tasks of guiding Jacob within the land of Israel and outside the land of Israel. Bethel is a liminal space, like Gilead, where the story of Elijah began.

Elijah's instruction to Elisha seems to be a curious non sequitur: why should the fact that YHWH has sent him to Bethel mean Elisha should stay where he is? Elisha's answer 'as YHWH lives' echoes Elijah's statement to Ahab at the beginning of the Elijah story, that of the widow of Zarephath to Elijah, the conversation between Elijah and Obadiah, and Micaiah's disclaimer to Ahab's messenger. But Elisha, representing Elijah's legacy (and your legacy) adds 'and as your soul lives', because he has grasped the non-duality of YHWH and Elijah, of *brahman* and *atman*.

> [3] The disciples of the prophets who were at Bethel came out to Elisha and said to him: 'Do you know that YHWH will take away your master from over you today?' And he said: 'Yes I know it. Be silent.'

Bethel is also the location of a group of prophets, or more literally 'sons of the prophets', a term that is used in some translations. The NRSV and some other translations call them a 'company of prophets', while the New JPS Tanakh and the God's Word Translation refer to them as 'disciples of the prophets', which I think is the most appropriate. It indicates they are prophets-in-training, apprentices, novices, as a bodhisattva is a buddha-in-training. It is noteworthy that they approach Elisha, as though he is their master, to speak to him about his master. Furthermore, they say Elijah will be taken away from *over* Elisha, but what matters is Elisha's *inner* teacher. There are parallels here with the guru-pupil relationship in Tibetan Buddhism, which is often misunderstood. At least one prominent Tibetan Buddhist teacher has said the guru is like a lighthouse, and you don't sail *toward* the lighthouse. Elijah and Elisha are portrayed as separate people, but if the inner teacher is going to depart, then who is left? Actually the inner teacher does not depart; rather, the pupil becomes one with the inner teacher, as Rumi became one with his teacher Shams. The prophets-in-training do not realize this yet, so Elisha tells them to be silent. Although their prophecy is true, it is misleading.

> [4] Elijah said to him: 'Elisha, please wait here, because YHWH has sent me to Jericho.' He replied: 'As YHWH lives and as your soul lives, I will not leave you.' So they went to Jericho, [5] and the disciples of the prophets who were at Jericho came near to Elisha and said to him: 'Do you know that YHWH will take away your master from over you today?' And he answered: 'Yes I know it. Be silent.'

The formula is repeated, but the place they go to is Jericho. This is another symbolic location—the beginning of Joshua's conquest, a 'returning to the source' in the language of the Zen ox-herding pictures. Again, it is a location of the disciples of the prophets. Do Elijah and Elisha go to these places because there are prophets-in-training there? Or are the prophets-in-training in those places because of their historic significance? It is natural to go to the place where it all began, and this might be inspirational, but in reality the Camino *begins* at Santiago—it is a new beginning, not a repeat of the old beginning.

> [6] *Elijah said to him: 'Please wait here, because YHWH has sent me to the Jordan.' And he said: 'As YHWH lives and as your soul lives, I will not leave you.' And they both went on.* [7] *Fifty disciples of the prophets went and stood opposite them at a distance, as they both stood by the Jordan.* [8] *Elijah took his mantle and wrapped it together. He struck the waters, and they were divided so that they both went over on dry ground.*

This time they really are going back to the source, to the liminal place, to the Jordan. And they cross over, they *exit* the land of Israel. For Elijah to be taken up into heaven he must *leave* the land of Israel. There are echoes of Moses here, but it is also a spiritual necessity. We can't attain nirvana if we cling to religious rituals and ceremonies, institutions, *conceptualizations* of ultimate truth (as Meister Eckhart realized when he prayed God to relieve him of God), a duality of us and them, believers and unbelievers, Buddhists and non-Buddhists, Christians and non-Christians...even nirvana itself. He can only find salvation outside the church—*nisi extra ecclesiam nulla salus*.

In Buddhism, 'the other shore' is sometimes used as a metaphor for enlightenment. But the Buddha also used it in a slightly different sense, with the story of a man on a journey who had to cross a river. To do so, he made a raft, and once he had crossed the river he left the raft where it was, rather than carrying it with him. Religious teachings and practices can be like that raft, useful for a time, but then an encumbrance if they are clung to. Another metaphor is that of a wall half-way up a mountain, and attached to that wall is a hoist that pulls people with amazing efficiency as far as the wall. Having got there, however, they find there is a wall in the way. Unfortunately, religious institutions have well-rehearsed arguments to discourage people from climbing over the wall, or leaving the raft behind.

The repetition of the number fifty from the previous chapter highlights a structural similarity, and also makes an allusion to the groups of fifty prophets who were hidden by Obadiah. Whether the fifty go from Jericho or from somewhere else is not clear, but they keep their distance, just as the disciples of the prophets had kept their distance from Elijah and only spoken to Elisha. They also keep their distance from the Jordan, indicating an attachment to the land of Israel that Elijah and Elisha are about to transcend. As Moses struck the Red Sea and Joshua struck the Jordan, so Elijah strikes the Jordan, but he uses his mantle. Earlier in the story, he threw his mantle on Elisha in a casual, off-hand way, instead of anointing him, but now this mantle symbolizes his spiritual attainment and his readiness to attain full enlightenment, to be free of all attachment.

Why cross the Jordan in this way? Taken literally it seems unnecessary, since there must have been boats around. When the Buddha heard of a man who had spent years developing the *siddhi* (magical power) of walking on water, he asked if there was a boatman nearby. He was told there was, and that the charge was one penny. So, said the Buddha, the value of this *siddhi* is one penny. (The crossing of rivers seems to be a theme in the Buddha's teaching.) But symbolically Elijah and Elisha's crossing is a demonstration of having transcended the attachment to place, and even attachment to the henotheistic understanding that God's place is in a particular territory. The medieval monk Hugo of St Victor said in his *Didascalicon* that those who consider their homeland sweet are still tender beginners, those to whom each country is as their native one are already strong, but to the perfect one each country is as a foreign land.

Elijah has frequently complained he is the only prophet of YHWH left, despite the evidence to the contrary. But now he realizes he is not the only one, and can happily pass on his mantle to Elisha.

> [9] *When they had gone over, Elijah said to Elisha: 'Ask what I shall do for you, before I am taken from you.' And Elisha said: 'Please let a double portion of your spirit be upon me.'*

Elijah acknowledges that Elisha knows he is about to be taken. His question seems almost polite, formal, but Elisha's response gets to the point. A double share could imply twice as much strength as Elijah, or a double share of the (spiritual) inheritance, as might go to a firstborn child, for example. It is like Solomon's request for wisdom, but unlike Solomon, Elisha doesn't even seem to consider the alternatives, such as wealth or long life.

> [10] *He said: 'You have asked a hard thing. Nevertheless, if you see me when I am taken from you, it will be as you ask, but if not, it will not be so.'*

It is a hard thing because spiritual insight and attainment cannot be inherited, yet the sharing of merit is more than just a ritual—if there is no self, then what is to stop merit from being transferred from one person to another? Karma must be understood within the context of *anatta*, not vice versa—so karma is that which is *experienced*, while *anatta* is that which is ontological.

Elijah's response is reminiscent of Buddhist teachings that link rebirth to the mind state immediately preceding death. Some examples of this are mythologically crude, such as the advanced practitioner whose last thought was of how beautiful a certain horse was and was consequently reborn as a horse, yet even these stories point to the importance of being prepared for death, and facing it with equanimity. It is not necessary to tell scary stories to make this point, but it is nonetheless a point worth making. Elisha has to keep his eyes on Elijah, maintain and develop single-pointed concentration, or, in more Sufi terms, have eyes only for one object, the Beloved.

[11] *As they continued on and talked, a chariot of fire and horses of fire appeared, which separated them from each other, and Elijah went up by a whirlwind into heaven.*

They continue walking and talking, and then the event happens, suddenly. The thing that triggers enlightenment can be minor—the words of a shopkeeper, a raised finger, the bottom falling out of a bucket of water.[1] It is a moment of sheer grace. Enlightenment does not come by seeking, yet only seekers find it.

The chariot of fire resembles the Zoroastrian king's chariot, and the fire motif that occurs throughout the story of Elijah may well be a reference to Zoroastrianism. But it is the fire that separates Elijah from Elisha—again, YHWH is not in the fire. In my very early years, a man in a nearby village lost his house and dog in a fire, and decided it was God's punishment for not going to church. So he started going, but one Sunday the minister (my father) read the verse 'YHWH was not in the fire', and this man shot up as though suddenly awakened. Apparently he kept going to church, but what matters is that he lost his view of YHWH as the jailer and hangman of his soul (to use Martin Luther's phrase[2]), and gained a new and better understanding.

Elijah is taken up in the whirlwind, where he gains not only a better understanding, but comes face-to-face with YHWH, what Buddhists call a direct perceptual realization of emptiness.

¹² Elisha saw it and cried: 'My father, my father, the chariots of Israel and its horsemen!' Then he saw him no more, and he took hold of his clothes and tore them in two pieces. ¹³ He also picked up the mantle of Elijah that fell from him.

Elisha continues watching—he maintains his single-pointed concentration, his oneness with the Beloved. His call 'My father, my father' is addressed to Elijah, but also emphasizes the allusion to the Zoroastrian king. It is pro-Cyrus in the late exilic or post-exilic context of the writing of the text, but it also suggests Israel is the equal of the Persian empire. Elisha's instinctive reaction is one of mourning. He tears his garment in two, which is seemingly dualistic. But Elisha has not been separated from his inner teacher, he has become one with his inner teacher. He really does inherit a double portion of Elijah's spirit, and this is confirmed by his picking up Elijah's mantle.

According to Sufi understanding: 'The goal of self-transformation is to remove all the veils between us and God. The final veil is the "I", the sense of separateness we each carry.'[3] In Elijah's case, this final veil has been removed, the final *klesha* has been transformed. His self has been annihilated, he has attained nirvana, he has become one with God. Yet, it is prophesied later in the Tanakh that he will return.[4] In the Gospels, Jesus refers to John the Baptist as 'the Elijah who is to come *if you can accept it*',[5] a tantalizing though strangely qualified implication that he is the *reincarnation* of Elijah. There are various stories of Elijah in Jewish tradition—including the Talmud—in which his political and spiritual roles are not separated, and the cup is left for him at the Passover table. He is even seen as a prototype of the

Buddha in later Jewish thought,[6] with another implied belief in some sort of reincarnation.

Many people view reincarnation (or rebirth) as a point of irreconcilable disagreement between Abrahamic and dharmic traditions, but this shows it is not alien to the former. Brueggemann insists that Elijah's ascension is a reminder not to fit the story into our ideas of rationality,[7] but past and future lives can be understood in a perfectly rational, even prosaic way. I am not referring to attempts to 'prove' rebirth with supposedly logical arguments, which have gone on in Buddhist circles for far too long. Some strands of Buddhism, especially Zen, regard rebirth as relatively unimportant. Following their example, I am not even referring to reincarnation as factually true or untrue. It is an *interpretation*.

Zen master Thich Nhat Hanh interprets rebirth using the imagery of a cloud.[8] A cloud seems to die when it empties itself of water, but in reality it has not died, it has been *transformed* into the water of a stream, or a river, or a glass of water, or even the sea. Similarly, when we die our bodies do not cease to exist; they are transformed, possibly into food for worms or ants, which then aerate the soil and help to provide food for other animals and humans. In a scientifically uncontroversial way, we are reborn in those people. As the eighteenth-century French scientist Lavoisier said: '*rien ne se perd, rien ne se crée, tout se transforme*'; nothing dies, nothing is born, everything changes.

What happens to our consciousness is harder to grasp, but we have seen that Elijah's consciousness was reincarnated in Elisha. That is what we mean when we say Elisha represents Elijah's legacy, and indeed the legacy of any seeker or questioner, including you and me. But unlike Elisha, a legacy does not have to be spectacular. There is a Tibetan story that the Buddha was reborn as a man, Mahasiddhi Thang Thong Gyalpo, who built many bridges and ferries, as well as temples, stupas and statues.[9] But we may simply be links in a chain, a good influence on just one other person, who in turn is a good influence on someone else, and so on. Somewhere along the chain, someone might have a transformative influence on many people. Legacy is reincarnation; the link is of the same substance as the chain.

In some schools of thought within Buddhism, it is hypothesized that there is a 'storehouse consciousness' (*alaya vijnana*), from which all of our experience derives and to which it all returns. In Yogachara/Chittamatra thought, which has influenced Zen, the *alaya* is seen as an individual phenomenon— it is one *alaya* per person. But it doesn't have to be seen that way; the *alaya* can legitimately be compared to Emile Durkheim's collective consciousness, or Carl Jung's collective *un*conscious. It means that everything we do, even the small things, really does affect the collective karma of humankind, and continues to do so over many generations. In some schools of Chinese and Japanese Buddhism, the *alaya* is seen as synonymous with the Buddha-nature, the *dharmadhatu*, the primordial nature, the primordial unity. What is this if it is not the ground of being, also known as YHWH? In this sense, the *alaya* is not subject to karma, but remember that karma is phenomenological, not ontological.[10]

If the Buddhist teachings on *anatta*—not-self—are valid then reincarnation cannot legitimately be understood individualistically. It often is, but that is because we forget the difference between phenomenology and ontology. It is like heaven and hell in Christian thought, which also should not be seen individualistically, but in terms of the line between good and evil that goes through the heart of every human being. Of course, heaven and hell have traditionally been seen as individual destinations—some people go to heaven and others go to hell—but this is hard to reconcile with some of Jesus' own teachings. Whatever you did for *one* of the least of these, you did it for me, he says to the sheep on his right who are admitted to eternal life. And whatever you did not do for *one* of the least of these, you did not do for me, he says to the goats on his left who are destined to eternal punishment.[11] Note the word 'one'. If there is anybody who is not a sheep *and* a goat by this measure, I have yet to meet that person.[12]

We are left with non-duality as telos. Eternity is the reconciliation of all contradictions, and nirvana is the extinction of all concepts, including self and not-self. We can compare this with the concept of omniscience. In Mahayana Buddhism the Buddha is portrayed as omniscient. Rather than divinizing the Buddha, as is sometimes claimed, this represents the belief that our very nature is to be omniscient, but this omniscience is obscured, as though by clouds which eventually clear away. However, a literal view of omniscience (applied to Buddha or God, when conceived as a being rather than the ground of being-itself) leads to logical contradictions. For example, would omniscient beings know how to keep secrets from themselves? A better view is to see omniscience firstly as a consequence of emptiness—to know everything is to know there is nothing to be known—and secondly as a consequence of non-duality—if there is no difference between me and others, neither is there a difference between what I know and what they know, and in that sense I can be said to know everything that is known. It is all in the *alaya*. When the Buddha sat down: 'He just sat down— in his own life, in his own mind, in his own condition, with his own karma—and aloneness was transformed. The whole world wasn't excluded; the dividing wall between his life, mind, condition and karma and that of the world was dropped.'[13]

Afterword: On Heresy

This book began with a saying attributed to Augustine, 'the more interpretations the better', and his insistence that any interpretation of the Bible that does not lead to a greater love of God and neighbor is a misinterpretation. However, Augustine was a harsh critic of doctrines he deemed heretical. My own interspiritual approach—though I believe it to be grounded in love of neighbor—is no doubt heretical in the eyes of many, and not just from the Christian tradition of Augustine.

Heresy is informally defined as 'wrong' doctrine, but this has not always been the case. In the story of Elijah, we have seen that the 'religious correctness' to which heresy is opposed is represented by Jehoshaphat, and it is a dry intellectual assent to doctrine with no inner transformation. But in the Gospels, it is said Jesus was *chosen* by God.[1] The Greek for 'chosen' is *hairetizo*, from which we get the words heresy, heretic, heretical, etc. So the teaching of the Gospels is that God is a heretic, and the relationship between God and Jesus is one of heresy! Of course, this is as far from the common use of the term as it is possible to get, but it is agreed by numerous ancient sources that the concept of heresy does indeed derive from the concept of choice, choosing what to believe instead of conforming to religious authority. If heresy means thinking for ourselves, then surely we all need to be heretics.

The pejorative use of the term has more in common with a different word used by Jesus in the Gospels, and that is the Aramaic word *raca*. Not only does Jesus warn his listeners against calling someone a *raca*, but he even suggests that doing so is worse than murder. So is the top-down anger we encountered in the story of Elijah, though none of them is quite as bad as calling someone a 'fool',[2] that is, someone who 'has said in their heart that there is no God', so an 'apostate' or 'infidel'. To state this as clearly as possible: murder is bad, anger is worse, calling someone a heretic is worse still, and calling someone an infidel is worst of all.

Early Christians don't seem to have been so cautious, but the arch-enemies were those thought to create division, *schisma* in Greek, rather than anyone who held a particular private theological opinion. In Buddhism, 'fomenting division in the sangha' is said to be one of the most karmically-negative things a person can do, alongside killing a parent, killing a bodhisattva, and wounding a Buddha. Of course, it takes two to start an argument, but this has rarely been acknowledged. The idea of heresy as a list of doctrinally unorthodox '-isms' seems to have taken root in the first few centuries of Christianity, but it can still be discerned in Augustine's *De Haeresibus* (c. 427–428) that the perceived problem related as much to orthopraxy as orthodoxy: the 'heresies' were allegedly leading people away from a love of God and neighbor, and even undermining their freedom. The modern understanding of 'cults' may give us a better idea of what Augustine was getting at. He was particularly appalled by the lack of forgiveness shown by the Donatists, though his denunciation of the Manichaeans seems more rooted in his own personal traumas.

We find the same dynamic in Buddhist history. The term 'heresy' is sometimes used in the same careless and uncaring way that it is in Christian circles. A more Buddhist term is 'wrong views'. Some translations of Buddhist texts use this to render the Pali *ditthi* or the Sanskrit *drsti*, but really these refer simply to 'views'. Even views—in this more general sense— are seen as problematic, because they are an obstacle to seeing things as they are, and can be a source of attachment. When we *identify* with our views, we suffer, as one Buddhist friend said to me. In *those* respects, there is no difference between a right view and a wrong view, even assuming we can objectively distinguish between them. 'Wrong view' better translates the

Pali *micchaditthi* and the Sanskrit *mithyadrsti*, which refer to views we *know* to be wrong but persist in holding anyway. A love for truth, a commitment to truth, means a willingness to face up to reality, even when we find it inconvenient. We have seen that truth is more than the avoidance of lies, but when we stop lying to *ourselves* then we really can speak the 'one word of truth' that Solzhenitsyn said 'outweighs the world'. Unfortunately, the tendency to conflate wrong views with particular doctrinal positions has taken root in Buddhism just as it has in Christianity, but the need to avoid *attachment* to views—including Buddhist ones—is still a part of Buddhist teaching and is emphasized by some Buddhist teachers, the best-known probably being Thich Nhat Hanh.[3]

What I am arguing is that terms like 'heresy' and 'wrong views' are sometimes deployed, even weaponized, in a way that forces people into a religious straitjacket. Heretics don't get burned at the stake any more, but the psychological pressure still does a damage of its own. Elias Hicks said:

How then shall we undertake to give a brother or a father a belief? If we do it, what wicked and presumptuous creatures we are, because we take the place of God. We assume the place of God when we tell our brother, this is the right way; my opinion is just right, and if thou do not come into it, thou art a heretic...Here now, contention and discord would enter, and every evil work prevail: but on the contrary, were they under the influence of brotherly love, they would be willing to say, each to the other, 'mind thy own business; thy Father hath given thee thy portion, and let it be what it may, be thou faithful. Do not mind me; I am not to be thy teacher; I am not to be an example to thee, any further than my example corresponds with what God commands thee to do.'[4]

To give someone else a belief is to begin from a *cataphatic* position, which is the opposite of the apophatic method that says, 'God is not this, God is not this.' With an apophatic spirit, a spirit of non-duality, we recognize that we see things differently, and say to each other all the same, 'be thou faithful'. As the Buddha said, you are your own teacher.[5] I wrote this book not because I have insights worth sharing, but because everyone is their own teacher. So be faithful to your own understanding, not to mine. If this commentary is successful, it will be a vehicle for your own thoughts, and those thoughts in turn will open up a diversity of perspectives and a wealth of spiritual resources, much of which I will be completely unaware of, and might even consider 'heretical'! The more interpretations that increase our love of the becoming possible of the impossible, and that help to reconcile our spiritual traditions, the better.

Appendix: Characters and Archetypes

The characters in the Elijah story do sometimes evolve, especially Ahab and Jezebel, so the cycle is not a simple *roman à clef* with each character representing a fixed archetype. Nonetheless, it is possible to find some pointers in the text. These are given in order of their appearance in the story:

Elijah—you, the seeker, the questioner.

Ahab—materialism, material security, power, duality, self-preservation, self-grasping, the need to conform, to be all things to all people, not challenging himself or others.

Ravens—impurity, the concept of which needs to be transcended.

Widow of Zarephath—humility, seeking for sticks in a forest (not seeing grace when it's in front of her), the temptation to give up.

Obadiah—relative *bodhicitta*, cf. Ananda or the Buddha's horse, the hesitancy of serving two masters being transformed into something more courageous and committed.

Jezebel—like Ahab: materialism, material security, power, duality; also greed, the temptress (note the sexism in the story here).

The prophets of Asherah—materialism, material comfort, self-preservation.

The prophets of Baal—dualism.

Elisha—your legacy.

Ben-hadad—anger, self-importance, sense of entitlement.

Naboth the Jezreelite—'the prophecies that YHWH sows', i.e. a rich communion with YHWH and speaking truth to power, and the connection between the two.

Jehoshaphat—'religious correctness', intellectual assent to doctrine without a genuine transformation.

Micaiah—in the place of Elijah, but as a third-person minor character allowing you (the seeker, the questioner) to see yourself in a decentered way.

Ahaziah—Ahab's legacy, the legacy of what Ahab represents, but who has no legacy of his own.

Endnotes

Introduction

1 Coventry Patmore, *Principle in Art, etc.*, George Bell and Sons, 1889, p. 44.

2 Nathan Katz, 'A Meeting of Ancient Peoples: Western Jews and the Dalai Lama of Tibet', 1991, http://www.jcpa.org/jl/hit20.htm.

3 *On Christian Doctrine*, book 1, chapter 36.

4 *On Religion*, Routledge, 2001, pp. 1–10.

5 E.g. *Christianity: Its Essence and History*, SCM Press, 1995, p. ii.

6 Quakerism is rooted in Christianity, while it is distinguished from other Christian traditions by an emphasis on the 'inner light', or 'that of God in everyone'. It is often self-defined by its core 'testimonies' of pacifism, integrity, simplicity, and equality.

7 *Living Buddha, Living Christ*, Riverhead, 1995, p. 11.

8 Number 2, https://qfp.quaker.org.uk/chapter/1/.

9 This is extensively and experientially described by Rodger Kamenetz in *Stalking Elijah: Adventures with Today's Jewish Mystical Masters*, HarperCollins, 1998.

10 'Toward a liberation theology of religions', in John Hick & Paul F. Knitter (eds), *The Myth of Christian Uniqueness. Toward a Pluralistic Theology of Religions*, Orbis, 1998, p. 187. See also his book *Without Buddha I Could Not Be a Christian*, Oneworld, 2009.

11 1 Corinthians 1:27–28.

12 *The Notebooks of Simone Weil*, Routledge, 2004, p. 228.

13 This is debated in Buddhism, but the principle is widely understood.

14 William J. Higginson with Penny Harter, *The Haiku Handbook*, Kodansha International, 1985, p. 195.

15   Jane Reichhold, *Writing and Enjoying Haiku*, Kodansha International, 2002, p. 125.

16   'Introduction', in *What Do We Do with the Bible?* SPCK, 2019, Kindle edition.

17   'What I Know from Kabbalah', https://www.beliefnet.com/faiths/judaism/2001/12/what-i-know-from-kabbalah.aspx.

18   Cf. C. Wright Mills's concept of 'the sociological imagination', in the classic 1959 book of that name.

19   Jewish Publication Society of America.

20   The verse numbering in Jewish Bibles occasionally differs slightly from that found in most Christian Bibles. Where that is the case, I have followed the Jewish numbering.

The Ground of Being (1 Kings 17)

1   I hesitated over whether or not to capitalize 'ground of being' and 'being-itself', but I decided not to, because it is not a title, nor is it something other-worldly; it is inseparable from everything that shares in being, including even the most mundane phenomena. According to Chuang Tzu (Zhuangzi), there is nowhere the Tao is not: it is in the ant, the weed, the common earthenware tile, even the dung.

2   *No Death, No Fear*, Riverhead, 2002, p. 32.

3   Genesis 32:23.

4   The New JPS Tanakh translates the text in Genesis 32:29 as 'beings divine and human'.

5   *Stalking Elijah*, p. 6.

6   *The Santiago Pilgrimage: Walking the Immortal Way*, MacLehose Press, 2016.

7   Job 38:41 (KJV).

8   Luke 3:11.

9   Judges 7:5–7.

10   Psalm 34:18.

11   *God of Love*, Monkfish, 2012, p. 149ff.

[12] 'Tonglen Meditation', http://www.beliefnet.com/Faiths/Faith-Tools/Meditation/1999/12/Tonglen-Meditation.aspx#i9jzsM7XvSlQhUDg.99.

[13] *The Hope: A Guide to Sacred Activism*, Hay House, 2009, p. 125.

[14] Paul Reps and Nyogen Senzaki, *Zen Flesh, Zen Bones*, Tuttle, 1988, p. 211.

[15] Acts 17:28.

[16] Qur'an 2:187.

[17] *A Buddhist Spectrum: Contributions to Buddhist–Christian Dialogue*, World Wisdom, 2003, pp. 65–69.

[18] Pallis, *A Buddhist Spectrum*, pp. 84–88.

[19] Shambhala, 1996, p. 17.

[20] 'Digging Deep to Holy Water', https://shalem.org/2009/01/14/digging-deep-to-holy-water.

[21] Quoted in Reynold A. Nicholson, *Studies in Islamic Mysticism*, 1921, p. 55 (reprinted by Curzon Press, Richmond, 1994).

[22] Pallis, *A Buddhist Spectrum*, pp. 160–161.

[23] *The Tibetan Book of Living and Dying*, Rider, 2008, p. 130.

[24] Annie Lionnet, *Secrets of Tarot*, Dorling Kindersley, 2001, p. 174.

[25] Matthew 18:3, 1 Peter 2:2, John 3:3. The phrase 'spiritual milk' can also be translated 'rational milk', 'metaphorical milk', 'milk of the *logos*', 'milk of the word', etc.

[26] Pallis, *A Buddhist Spectrum*, p. 170.

[27] Shunryu Suzuki, *Zen Mind, Beginner's Mind*, Shambhala, 2011, p. 1.

Samsara (1 Kings 18:1–19)

[1] Mainly by conservative Evangelical writers, but this in itself does not invalidate the point.

[2] *Aion: Researches into the Phenomenology of the Self*, Princeton University Press, 1969, p. 89.

3   Luke 18:13 (KJV).

4   Brandon Toropov and Chadwick Hansen, *The Complete Idiot's Guide to Taoism*, Alpha Books, 2002, p. 112.

5   Genesis 13:11.

6   *Advices and Queries*, number 35, https://qfp.quaker.org.uk/chapter/1/.

7   Genesis 17:3, 19:1.

8   Psalm 51:4.

9   Romans 14:23.

10 *Let Your Life Speak*, Jooey-Bass, 2000, pp. 64, 88.

11 'The Spirituality of the Future', https://theshalomcenter.org/node/1395.

12 Logion 77.

13 'Dona Sutta: With Dona', n. 2, https://www.accesstoinsight.org/tipitaka/an/an04/an04.036.than.html.

14 See for example *Zen Flesh, Zen Bones*, p. 186.

15 Parker Palmer, as paraphrased in Rory McEntee and Adam Bucko, *The New Monasticism: An Interspiritual Manifesto for Contemplative Living*, Orbis, 2015, p. 105.

16 *Either/Or* and *Fear and Trembling*, both available in several editions.

17 2 Kings 2:25.

18 Indeed, the 'prophets' (*neviim*) and 'priests' (*kohanim*) of Baal are explicitly distinguished from each other in 2 Kings 10:19, and it is only the prophets who are mentioned in the story of Elijah.

19 'From Western Marxism to Western Buddhism: The Taoist Ethic and the Spirit of Global Capitalism', *Cabinet Magazine*, 2, 2001, https://www.cabinetmagazine.org/issues/2/zizek.php.

The *Kleshas* (1 Kings 18:20–40)

1   Amos 9:3.

2   *I and Thou*, Continuum, 2004, p. 61ff.

3   John 14:6. Sadly, this beautiful verse is routinely misrepresented as a claim to Christian exclusivity.

4   Footnote to this verse in the New JPS Tanakh; Francis Brown et al., *A Hebrew and English Lexicon of the Old Testament*, Clarendon, 1907, p. 704.

5   Jeffrey Hopkins, *Meditation on Emptiness*, Wisdom Publications, 1996, p. 258.

6   Mark 12:41–44, Luke 21:1–4.

7   e.g. Psalm 2:4.

8   This threefold distinction is common in humor studies. It seems to derive from John Morreall in *The Philosophy of Laughter and Humor* (State University of New York Press, 1987), though of course the theories themselves go back much further. I find it interesting that philosophers of the stature of Aristotle, Kant and Freud have written about humor, suggesting it shouldn't be seen as a trivial topic.

9   'Homilies on the Gospel of Matthew', Homily 6, §8.

10   Quoted in Ron Ferguson's biography, *George Mackay Brown: The Wound and the Gift*, Saint Andrew Press, 2011, p. xxii.

11   *Redeeming Laughter*, Walter de Gruyter, 2014.

12   Penguin, 1971.

13   Quoted in Rodger Kamenetz, *The Jew in the Lotus*, HarperCollins, 1995, p. 28.

14   *Zen Mind, Beginner's Mind*, pp. 110–111.

15   *Let Your Life Speak*, p. 10.

16   Martin Buber, *Tales of the Hasidim*, Schocken Books, 2011, Kindle edition.

17   John Stevens, *The Marathon Monks of Mount Hiei*, Shambhala, 1988, pp. 84, 128, 148.

18   e.g. Matthew 13:46, Luke 14:33.

19   Luke 7:38, John 12:3.

20   Pico Iyer, *The Open Road: The Global Journey of the Fourteenth Dalai Lama*, Viking, 2008, p. 143.

21   Matthew 11:14, 3:11; Luke 3:16.

22 He wrote this on a piece of paper which he sewed into his clothing; it was found after his death.

23 'What I Know from Kabbalah', https://www.beliefnet.com/faiths/judaism/2001/12/what-i-know-from-kabbalah.aspx.

24 Buber, *I and Thou*, passim.

25 Reynold Nicholson's translation, book 2, line 1762 (public domain). Coleman Barks keeps the same wording.

26 Exodus 13:21–22.

27 *Fear and Trembling*, chapter 2.

28 Overlook Press, 1998, p. 130.

29 Judges 4–5.

30 Nazir 23b:7.

31 Sanhedrin 96b, Gittin 57b.

The Liminal Stage (1 Kings 18:41–19:9a)

1 e.g. 'Brother Roger's Unfinished Letter', https://www.taize.fr/en_article2964.html.

2 *The Power of the Name: The History and the Practices of the Jesus Prayer*, Orthodox Research Institute, 2008, p. 38.

3 From the story of Hyakujo's fox in *Zen Flesh, Zen Bones*, pp. 129–130.

4 'What Jesus Runs Away From', in *The Essential Rumi*, HarperCollins, 2004, p. 204.

5 Book 3, line 2570ff.

6 Psalm 14:1, 53:2.

7 Many translations go even further and write 'the gods' with a lower-case g, but the Hebrew does not have upper and lower case.

8 From Gregory Palamas, cited in Karen Armstrong, *The Great Transformation*, Alfred A. Knopf, 2006, p. 393.

9 Alan J. Hauser, 'Yahweh Versus Death: The Real Struggle in 1 Kings 17–19', in Alan J. Hauser (ed.), *From Carmel to Horeb: Elijah in Crisis*, Almond, 1990, p. 64; Dan Epp-Tiessen, '1 Kings 19: The Renewal of Elijah', *Direction*,

35(1), 2006, http://www.directionjournal.org/35/1/1-kings-19-renewal-of-elijah.html.

10   *The Gateless Gate*, Wisdom Publications, 2004, pp. 183–184.

11   Numbers 13:2,25.

12   1 Samuel 17:16.

13   Deuteronomy 9:11,25, 10:10.

14   Matthew 4:2, Mark 1:13, Luke 4:2, Acts 1:3.

15   Kamenetz, *Stalking Elijah*, p. 17. The four worlds are sometimes named differently, e.g. action, formation, creation, and emanation.

Not in the Fire (1 Kings 19:9b–21)

1   Jeremiah 20:7. Most translations say 'deceived' rather than 'seduced'; I first came across this variant translation in the film *Into Great Silence*.

2   See for example Hopkins, *Meditation on Emptiness*, pp. 134, 286.

3   *Living Buddha, Living Christ*, p. 14ff.

4   E.g. *Where There Is Love, There Is God*, Doubleday, 2010, passim.

5   It is because non-duality is apophatic that I have chosen to hyphenate it — the emphasis is quite deliberately on what it is *not*, not on what it is.

6   2 Kings 8:10–13, 9:6.

7   Pallis, *A Buddhist Spectrum*, pp. 201–202.

8   2 Samuel 24:21–25.

Anger (1 Kings 20)

1   *Zen Flesh, Zen Bones*, p. 86.

2   See Buber, *I and Thou*.

3   Hopkins, *Meditation on Emptiness*, p. 256; Asanga, *Abhidharmasamuccaya: The Compendium of the Higher Teaching Philosophy by Asanga*, translated by Sara Boin-Webb, Jain Publishing, 2001, pp. 11–12 n. 20.

4   *No Death, No Fear*, p. 32.

5   1 Kings 15.

6   Matthew 5:22.

7   Matthew 21:12–13; Mark 11:15–17; Luke 19:45–46; John 2:14–16.

8   For example, H.H. the Dalai Lama, Tsong-ka-pa and Jeffrey Hopkins, *Tantra in Tibet*, Snow Lion, 1987, p. 112.

9   Walter Brueggemann, *1 & 2 Kings*, Smyth & Helwys, 2000, pp. 246–247.

10   1 Corinthians 1:27–28.

11   Sexual misconduct is undefined in the earliest Buddhist teachings, but I find 'harmful sex' a more plausible interpretation than the legalistic and homophobic interpretations of later commentators. *Quaker Faith and Practice* (22.11) says, 'No relationship can be a right one which makes use of another person through selfish desire' (https://qfp.quaker.org.uk/passage/22-11/). Lying, in the Buddhist sense, can also encompass harsh and angry speech.

12   Exodus 12:2 suggests spring, while Exodus 23:16 suggests autumn.

13   Cf. John 10:16.

14   Joshua 6:3–16.

15   Joshua 6:1,20–21.

16   *The Gulag Archipelago* (abridged edition), Perennial Classics, 2002, p. 75.

17   A more literal rendering of Rumi would be beyond disbelief/infidelity and Islam/submission.

18   *A Series of Extemporaneous Discourses*, 1825, pp. 164, 166.

19   *Resistance, Rebellion, and Death*, Alfred A. Knopf, 1966, p. 199.

20   Tony Benn said that politicians can be weathervanes or signposts—he advocated being a signpost.

21   *The Great Transformation*, p. 87.

22   *Buddha*, Weidenfeld & Nicolson, 2000, pp. 49–50.
23   *Stages of Faith*, HarperCollins, 1981, p. 200.
24   Cf. 2 Samuel 17:10.
25   E.g. Matthew 8:28, Mark 1:34, 3:11.
26   Matthew 6:14–15, 7:1–2.

The Politics of *Anatta* (1 Kings 21)

1   Brueggemann, *1 & 2 Kings*, p. 202.
2   *The Shock Doctrine: The Rise of Disaster Capitalism*, Knopf, 2007.
3   Jeffery Paine, *Re-enchantment: Tibetan Buddhism Comes to the West*, Norton, 2004, pp. 76–77.
4   *A Series of Extemporaneous Discourses*, p. 164.
5   Muwatta Imam Malik, book 15, hadith 7.
6   *An Essay on the Development of Christian Doctrine*, 1845, p. 39.
7   Brueggemann, *1 & 2 Kings*, p. 261.
8   Geza Vermes, *The Complete Dead Sea Scrolls in English*, Penguin, 2004, p. 180.
9   Matthew 5:3.
10   1 Timothy 6:10.
11   Matthew 6:16–18.

The Lies of God (1 Kings 22)

1   2 Chronicles 18:1–3.
2   Ruth 1:16.
3   *The Interior Castle*, 1588 (available in several English translations), sixth mansion, Chapter 3.
4   Ruth 3:6–9.
5   Hopkins, *Meditation on Emptiness*, p. 253.
6   Genesis 2:17, 3:3,6.
7   Isaiah 45:6–7.

8   e.g. Ghorban Elmi, 'Ahmad Ghazali's Satan', *HTS Theological Studies*, 75(3), 2019, http://dx.doi.org/10.4102/hts.v75i3.5368. Ghazali used the Arabic *zindiq*, not *kafir* or *mushrik*.

9   David O'Neal (ed.), *Meister Eckhart, From Whom God Hid Nothing: Sermons, Writings, and Sayings*, New Seeds, 2005, p. 72.

10 John 7:8–10.

11 Lotus Sutra, Chapter 3. This sutra may be the most divisive Buddhist text. It is not part of the Theravada canon; its one-vehicle (*ekayana*) teaching is regarded as metaphorical by some Mahayana sects and definitive by others; and it is regarded as the pinnacle of the Buddha's teaching in Nichiren Buddhism, whose adherents chant *nam myoho renge kyo* (homage to the Lotus Sutra of the true dharma) many times a day.

12 The Long String', in *The Essential Rumi*, p. 81.

The Labyrinth and the Mandala (2 Kings 1)

1   'De Servo Arbitrio "On the Enslaved Will" or The Bondage of Will', 1524, section IV, https://ccel.org/ccel/luther/bondage/bondage.

2   'The Jesus Hermeneutic', in *What Do We Do with the Bible?*, Kindle edition.

3   'Is Buddhism Really Nontheistic?', *Snow Lion*, 15(1), 2000, pp. 1, 12–13.

4   p. 105.

5   John 12:24. Fans of Dostoevsky will recognize this as the quote at the beginning of *The Brothers Karamazov*.

6   *Love and Living*, Farrar, Straus and Giroux, 1979, p. 10.

7   *Zen Flesh, Zen Bones*, p. 88.

8   See for example *Quaker Faith and Practice*, 20.27–20.36, https://qfp.quaker.org.uk/passage/20-27/.

9   *Zen Flesh, Zen Bones*, pp. 48–49.

Enlightenment (2 Kings 2:1–13a)

1   *Zen Flesh, Zen Bones*, pp. 48–49, 50, 119–120.

2   James Kittelson, *Luther the Reformer*, Augsburg Fortress Publishing House, 1986, p. 79.

3   James Fadiman & Robert Frager, in *Essential Sufism*, HarperSanFrancisco, 1999, p. 243.

4   Malachi 4:5.

5   Matthew 11:14.

6   Emil G. Hirsch et al., 'Elijah', *The Jewish Encyclopedia*, 1906, https://www.jewishencyclopedia.com/articles/5634-elijah#anchor14.

7   *1 & 2 Kings*, p. 296.

8   *No Death, No Fear*, pp. 25–26.

9   Usually the Buddha is said to have entered nirvana and not been reborn.

10   Karl Brunnhölzl, *In Praise of Dharmadhatu: Nāgārjuna and the Third Karmapa, Rangjung Dorje*, Snow Lion Publications, 2007, pp. 49–50; Thomas McEvilley, *The Shape of Ancient Thought: Comparative Studies in Greek and Indian Philosophies*, Allsworth Press, 2002, chapter 23 passim (Kindle edition).

11   Matthew 25:31–46.

12   This seems to me a legitimate interpretation of Karl Barth's understanding of the subject, and indeed of the whole Calvinist tradition within Christianity. I cannot hope to elucidate a comment like this without devoting (at least) a whole chapter to the subject, but some of my thinking has been stimulated by Alastair McIntosh's book *Island Spirituality*, The Islands Book Trust, 2013, which I recommend. It is out of print and can legally be downloaded from his website at http://www.alastairmcintosh.com/islandspirituality.htm.

13   Bonnie Myotei Treace, 'Afterword: Hermitage Heart', in John Stevens [translator], *Lotus Moon: The Poetry of Rengetsu*, White Pine Press, 2005, p. 128.

Afterword: On Heresy

1 Matthew 12:18.

2 Matthew 5:21–22.

3 Especially in *Interbeing: The 14 Mindfulness Trainings of Engaged Buddhism* (4th edition), Parallax Press, 2020.

4 *A Series of Extemporaneous Discourses*, pp. 172–173. Elias Hicks did use male-centered language—he was alive from 1748 to 1830—but the phrase 'a brother or a father' alludes to the earlier part of this discourse, which can be found online. Quakers continued to use 'thee' and 'thy' (and to a lesser extent 'thou') well into the twentieth century, regarding them as more egalitarian and less ostentatious than 'you' and 'your', which in the seventeenth century were used for social superiors, a concept to which Quakers were (and are) opposed.

5 *Dhammapada*, 12:4 (160). The Pali word *nātho* is variously translated as teacher, Lord, master, refuge, destiny, protector, etc.

Select Bibliography

Armstrong, Karen (2000), *Buddha*, Weidenfeld & Nicolson.

— (2006), *The Great Transformation*, Alfred A. Knopf.

Asanga (2001), *Abhidharmasamuccaya: The Compendium of the Higher Teaching Philosophy by Asanga* (translated by Sara Boin-Webb), Jain Publishing.

Britain Yearly Meeting (Society of Friends) (2009), *Quaker Faith and Practice* (5th edition), Quaker Home Service (also available online).

Brueggemann, Walter (2000), *1 & 2 Kings*, Smyth & Helwys.

Brunnhölzl, Karl (2007), *In Praise of Dharmadhatu: Nāgārjuna and the Third Karmapa, Rangjung Dorje*, Snow Lion Publications.

Buber, Martin (2004), *I and Thou*, Continuum.

— (2011), *Tales of the Hasidim*, Schocken Books.

Caputo, John (2001), *On Religion*, Routledge.

Fowler, James W. (1981), *Stages of Faith*, HarperCollins.

Goettmann, Alphonse and Goettmann, Rachel (2008), *The Power of the Name: The History and the Practices of the Jesus Prayer*, Orthodox Research Institute.

Hauser, Alan J. (ed.) (1990), *From Carmel to Horeb: Elijah in Crisis*, Almond.

Hick, John and Knitter, Paul F. (eds) (1988), *The Myth of Christian Uniqueness. Toward a Pluralistic Theology of Religions*, Orbis.

Hicks, Elias (1825), *A Series of Extemporaneous Discourses*, Joseph and Edward Parker (available online).

Hopkins, Jeffrey (1996), *Meditation on Emptiness*, Wisdom Publications.

Kamenetz, Rodger (1995), *The Jew in the Lotus*, HarperCollins.

— (1998), *Stalking Elijah: Adventures with Today's Jewish Mystical Masters*, HarperCollins.

Knitter, Paul F. (2009), *Without Buddha I Could Not Be a Christian*, Oneworld.

Küng, Hans (1995), *Christianity: Its Essence and History*, SCM Press.

McEntee Rory and Bucko, Adam (2015), *The New Monasticism: An Interspiritual Manifesto for Contemplative Living*, Orbis.

McEvilley, Thomas (2002), *The Shape of Ancient Thought: Comparative Studies in Greek and Indian Philosophies*, Allsworth Press.

McIntosh, Alastair (2013), *Island Spirituality*, The Islands Book Trust.

O'Neal, David (ed.) (2005), *Meister Eckhart, From Whom God Hid Nothing: Sermons, Writings, and Sayings*, New Seeds.

Paine, Jeffery (2004), *Re-enchantment: Tibetan Buddhism Comes to the West*, Norton.

Pallis, Marco (2003), *A Buddhist Spectrum: Contributions to Buddhist–Christian Dialogue*, World Wisdom.

Palmer, Parker (2000), *Let Your Life Speak*, Jooey-Bass.

Reps, Paul & Senzaki, Nyogen (1988), *Zen Flesh, Zen Bones*, Tuttle.

Rohr, Richard (2019), *What Do We Do with the Bible?*, SPCK.

Starr, Mirabai (2012), *God of Love: A Guide to the Heart of Judaism, Christianity, and Islam*, Monkfish.

Suzuki, Shunryu (2011), *Zen Mind, Beginner's Mind*, Shambhala.

Thich Nhat Hanh (1995), *Living Buddha, Living Christ*, Riverhead.

— (2002), *No Death, No Fear*, Riverhead.

— (2020), *Interbeing: The 14 Mindfulness Trainings of Engaged Buddhism* (4th edition), Parallax Press.

Wallace, B. Alan (2000), 'Is Buddhism Really Nontheistic?', *Snow Lion*, vol. 15, no. 1, pp. 1, 12–13.

Yamada, Kōun (2004), *The Gateless Gate*, Wisdom Publications.

A Note to the Reader

Thank you so much for your interest in this book. I think it was the great Anon who said 'speak your truth, find your tribe', and that's at least part of what I'm trying to do here. So, if you found this book enjoyable, thought-provoking, puzzling or something I would never in a million years think of, please leave an honest review somewhere, tell your friends, and feel free to get in touch. Sometimes I prefer pictures to words, so you can find me at www.instagram.com/mdbauthorpage.

O-BOOKS

SPIRITUALITY

O is a symbol of the world, of oneness and unity; this eye
represents knowledge and insight. We publish titles on general
spirituality and living a spiritual life. We aim to inform and
help you on your own journey in this life.
If you have enjoyed this book, why not tell other readers
by posting a review on your preferred book site?

Recent bestsellers from O-Books are:

Heart of Tantric Sex
Diana Richardson
Revealing Eastern secrets of deep love and intimacy
to Western couples.
Paperback: 978-1-90381-637-0 ebook: 978-1-84694-637-0

Crystal Prescriptions
The A-Z guide to over 1,200 symptoms and their healing crystals
Judy Hall
The first in the popular series of eight books, this handy little
guide is packed as tight as a pill bottle with crystal remedies
for ailments.
Paperback: 978-1-90504-740-6 ebook: 978-1-84694-629-5

Shine On
David Ditchfield and J S Jones
What if the aftereffects of a near-death experience were undeniable? What if a person could suddenly produce high-quality paintings of the afterlife, or if they acquired the ability to compose classical symphonies? Meet: David Ditchfield.
Paperback: 978-1-78904-365-5 ebook: 978-1-78904-366-2

The Way of Reiki
The Inner Teachings of Mikao Usui
Frans Stiene
The roadmap for deepening your understanding of the system of Reiki and rediscovering your
True Self.
Paperback: 978-1-78535-665-0 ebook: 978-1-78535-744-2

You Are Not Your Thoughts.
Frances Trussell
The journey to a mindful way of being, for those who want to truly know the power of mindfulness.
Paperback: 978-1-78535-816-6 ebook: 978-1-78535-817-3

The Mysteries of the Twelfth Astrological House
Fallen Angels
Carmen Turner-Schott, MSW, LISW
Everyone wants to know more about the most misunderstood house in astrology — the twelfth astrological house.
Paperback: 978-1-78099-343-0 ebook: 978-1-78099-344-7

WhatsApps from Heaven
Louise Hamlin
An account of a bereavement and the extraordinary
signs — including WhatsApps — that a retired
law lecturer received from her deceased husband.
Paperback: 978-1-78904-947-3 ebook: 978-1-78904-948-0

The Holistic Guide to Your Health
& Wellbeing Today
Oliver Rolfe
A holistic guide to improving your complete health,
both inside and out.
Paperback: 978-1-78535-392-5 ebook: 978-1-78535-393-2

Cool Sex
Diana Richardson and Wendy Doeleman
For deeply satisfying sex, the real secret is to reduce the heat,
to cool down. Discover the empowerment and fulfilment
of sex with loving mindfulness.
Paperback: 978-1-78904-351-8 ebook: 978-1-78904-352-5

Creating Real Happiness A to Z
Stephani Grace
Creating Real Happiness A to Z will help you understand
the truth that you are not your ego
(conditioned self).
Paperback: 978-1-78904-951-0 ebook: 978-1-78904-952-7

A Colourful Dose of Optimism
Jules Standish
It's time for us to look on the bright side, by boosting
our mood and lifting our spirit, both in our interiors,
as well as in our closet.
Paperback: 978-1-78904-927-5 ebook: 978-1-78904-928-2

Readers of ebooks can buy or view any of these bestsellers by
clicking on the live link in the title. Most titles are published
in paperback and as an ebook. Paperbacks are available in
traditional bookshops. Both print and ebook formats are
available online.

Find more titles and sign up to our readers' newsletter at
www.o-books.com

Follow O books on Facebook at **O-books**

For video content, author interviews and more, please subscribe to our YouTube channel:

O-BOOKS Presents

Follow us on social media for book news, promotions and more:

Facebook: O-Books

Instagram: @o_books_mbs

Twitter: @obooks

Tik Tok: @ObooksMBS

www.o-books.com